Small Footprint

how to live simply and love extravagantly

Big Handprint

tri robinson

Small Footprint

how to live simply and love extravagantly

Big Handprint

tri robinson

ampelōn

PUBLISHING

Boise, ID

ISBN: 978-0-9786394-8-8
Printed in the United States of America
First printing

Requests for information should be addressed to:
Ampelon Publishing
PO Box 140675
Boise, ID 83714

For other Ampelon Publishing products, visit us on the web at: www.ampelonpublishing.com

Cover design: Lisa Dyches — cartwheelstudios.com

To the amazing people who make up the fellowship of the Vineyard of Boise. You have made the past twenty years of my pastorate a rich, joyous and a never-ending adventure.

Contents

acknowledgements 9

introduction 11

chapter one: small footprint 15
rendering down our lives

chapter two: big handprint 27
making a lasting positive impact

chapter three: pathway to adventure 41
seizing opportunity at every turn

chapter four: a simple solution 53
the answer to two daunting commissions

chapter five: less external complexity 67
how our stuff creates barriers to leaving a big handprint

chapter six: less internal complexity 81
making more room for God to work

chapter seven: more preparedness 99
being ready creates opportunity for bigger handprints

conclusion: beyond the big handprint...................................115
reform yourself and your church ... or languish in irrelevance

notes 127

discussion guide 131

Acknowledgments

At the end of 2006 during a time of solitude, I asked the Lord for fresh direction so I might effectively lead our church into a new year. It was then that I received a clear picture of a word in a way that I had never seen it before. The word was "advent-ure" with a hyphen separating *advent* and *ure*. I had a strong sense that I was to challenge people to pursue the only true adventure—living a life of courageous, radical and daring faith between the first and second "advent" (or *coming*) of Jesus. The "advent-ure" has become for us a call to a different kind of life; a life that can only be manifested after an awakening to the reality that the Kingdom of God has come to earth. In telling this story, I must acknowledge my creative staff, our committed leaders and the many participants at the Vineyard of Boise who are increasingly choosing this unique lifestyle. If not for them, I would have no credence to write this book. Their many stories are the credibility that will back the challenge for anyone who dares to live their life in such a way to make a smaller footprint on this earth in the hopes of making a bigger handprint on humanity.

introduction

Perhaps it was because I gave my life to Christ in the heat of the Jesus movement during the 1970s; or maybe it was because as a young Christian I sat under the teaching of men who had a radically different idea about how we were to live our lives as followers of Jesus; or quite possibly it was just the way God wired me from the beginning. Whatever the reason, I have never believed the Christian life was something to be lived out in passivity. I have always considered it to be a "verb," something that was meant to show action as a state of being. My wife Nancy and I have always considered the life of faith to be a great adventure, and we have tried to live it and preach it accordingly for over 25 years.

Not long ago, I was having lunch at a favorite little Mexican restaurant here in Boise with a friend, Greg Prosch. Over the past seven years, Greg and his wife Sharon have taken a role of active leadership in our church. They both graduated from an intensive two-year seminary-level training program our church offers. Sharon has served faithfully for years as a youth leader, and Greg has a major leadership responsibility in the training program. Together, they have also overseen our marriage ministries in the church.

Greg and Sharon aren't what you would call new kids on the block, or even those who are still considering what to do in the church. They are fully committed to the Christian life—in the saddle, tried and proven. Yet, lately Greg has been restless and unsettled; he has wanted to do more with his life. Through the world's eyes Greg has it made. He has a wife that is willing to go to the ends of the earth with him. He has a teenage son who he loves very much. He has a successful career, holding a management position at a major computer corporation with a better-than-average salary package. He is very personable, sharp-looking and well-educated. In so many ways, Greg has it made. But that day as we ate lunch together, he talked about craving to do more with his life. Greg had tasted the Kingdom of God, participated in it, and wouldn't settle for anything less.

Around the time I met with Greg I had been teaching a series called "The Adventure", challenging people to live an authentic Christian life. "The Adventure" is a call to a unique and even peculiar lifestyle between the first and second advent of Jesus. It presents a challenge to live a life of radical faith. It illuminates the fact that God's Kingdom has come to earth even as it is in heaven with the first coming of Jesus—and yet, it hasn't come close to the fullness it will be in His second coming. It is the acknowledgement that we live in a very unique time in human history, a time that needs a people who are willing to use their faith to impact a world crying out for help. It is a time that requires a people who have accepted the Gospel and are willing to break status-quo living. Greg and Sharon Prosch took that challenge.

Greg was faced with the huge decision that every Christian who truly desires to break free into a life of effective ministry faces. He and Sharon, like so many others, were at a crossroad. Greg's life had become too complex and encumbered to give him the freedom to do more than he was doing for Christ. He and Sharon owned a wonderful home and had a comfortable lifestyle. Unfortunately, some unwise financial choices and unexpected circumstances in life had them facing a huge debt load that was holding them temporarily captive. Because of this, the majority of Greg's earning power went to cover that debt. I challenged Greg to sit down with Sharon and together develop a seven-year plan that would enable them to downsize their life so that they could upsize their effectiveness in the world they so desired to impact.

Complexity comes in many forms; it can be monetary as in Greg's case, but it can also be emotional, spiritual or relational, all of which can be far more debilitating than having financial struggles. Material possessions, such as the expensive toys that once promised to enrich our lives, have a way of owning us with payments and often even stimulate guilt when they are taking up space in our closets, garages or driveways. Most Americans have too much stuff; stuff that often weighs them down and ultimately keeps them from a more simplified, freeing life.

Years ago as a young man I saw a sign at a trailhead that led into the back country of the Sierra Nevada Mountains in the Inyokern National Forest. It read, "Leave only footprints—take only pictures." This statement has been indelible on my mind through the years as I have hiked and horse-packed into the backcountry of the western states. It became vital to me from that day forward that I leave as little evidence as possible when I venture into the majestic mountains and wilderness or the pristine lakes and valleys. On the other hand I realized I could take with me something of great value. I could take with me the rich memories of being with family and friends in places yet unblemished by the lasting imprints of a developing society. This thought began to translate into other parts of my life. It became my goal to leave a smaller footprint with my life and a bigger handprint of God.

There has been much talk lately about a person's "carbon footprint." This refers to the lasting impact one person makes in their lifetime of living on planet Earth. It is determined by the fuels we burn, the non-renewable resources we consume and the pollution we produce. The size of your carbon footprint is dependent on things such as the size of vehicle you drive, the expanse and efficiency of the home you inhabit and the waste you left behind. The size of your carbon footprint will dictate the blessings or struggles for future generations because of your impact on the earth's condition after your life has passed.

Because a small footprint—a life of simplicity—is a life that prioritizes, downsizes and slows its pace, it is a life that has the potential to accomplish much while still using less. It is a life that cares about humanity and the earth's generations to come. Our desire should be to leave a small human footprint but a large and lasting handprint of God. The handprint we leave is an imprint on the hearts and memories of the people whose lives we touch.

A few months after our first meeting, Greg and I returned to the same hole-in-the-wall Mexican restaurant for a follow up. He shared with me the seven-year plan he and Sharon had developed to put them in a position of freedom. They decided together that they desired a life of united ministry without the restraints of debilitating debt. They wanted to make a difference in the world with the life they had been given. They set realistic goals, knowing that in order to achieve them they would have to make sacrifices and lifestyle changes. They would have to downsize their life so that they might upsize their effectiveness. They were obviously serious and committed to the ideal that many Christians are now beginning to share—one of leaving a smaller footprint so they might also leave a bigger handprint on the lives and world around them.

chapter one

Small Footprint

Rendering down our lives

"This ain't my American dream. I want to live and
die for bigger things."
– Jonathan Foreman of the band Switchfoot

Begin using your hands for honest work, and then give
generously to others in need.
– Ephesians 4:28

I don't know how it happened, especially since I never intended it to happen. I just woke up one morning with the realization that I was tired. Not the kind of tired where you didn't get enough sleep the previous night, but the kind of tired where you boldly proclaim to anyone who will listen, "I need a vacation." Somehow life had gotten away from me and for the past several years I had been chasing after it, unable to accomplish half of what I had desired to do. In so many areas of my life I had been spinning my wheels, unable to delineate the most important from the somewhat important. Sitting on various boards, building a wonderful growing church body that I loved in Boise, constructing a mountain cabin with my family, as well as maintaining my country home and ranch with my wife Nancy—it all seemed most important.

On a case-by-case basis, everything seemed like it belonged on the top shelf of my life's priorities. As a regional director, I oversaw nearly a hundred churches in nine states. I traveled across the country and around the world teaching seminars, conferences and encouraging and training church leaders. I was a grandparent, a parent, a husband and a son to people I deeply cared about and who deeply cared about me. I was juggling a hundred balls, not wanting any of them to drop—and I was tired. That morning as I looked out my front window at the distant snow-capped mountains, I realized something had to give. My life had become too complex, too busy and too out-of-control. I realized that the great things that truly gave me joy and the things I deeply desired to invest my life in were being pushed aside for dozens of merely good things. Not just good things but important things—things I had felt privileged to be a part of. It was time for reevaluation, reorganization and refocus.

That year both of Nancy's parents had passed away—and amidst the mourning and sense of loss, the realization that "life is short" hit us both. It was like the psalmist once said, "You have made my days a mere handbreadth; the span of my years is as nothing before you.

Each man's life is but a breath" (Psalm 39:5, NIV). Our lives had clearly grown too complex.

Deep within all of us, we have yearned for a life rendered down to God's good, pleasing and perfect will, lives that weren't traveling at such breakneck speeds that they missed the very gift of life itself. This is neither the life we aspired to nor the life we signed up for. Where is the peace? The sheer joy in life? The pursuit of something great, not simply something good enough?

On Walden Pond

When Nancy and I met near the end of the 1960s, our culture was experiencing major transitions and shifts. No aspect of our life seemed exempt from these changes. Centered in the Baby Boomer generation, I noticed everyone was looking for answers concerning morality, world peace, an uncertain future and the meaning of life itself. The environment had zoomed to the forefront of our social issues because of its rapidly degenerating condition. We were scared and didn't know what to do about it. Few people in our generation had any working knowledge of biblical truth and as a result couldn't receive any comfort from knowing that there was a Creator who was still very much in control.

Rather than looking to God for answers, we read authors and poets like Ralph Waldo Emerson, Walt Whitman and Henry David Thoreau. In an out-of-control, complex world, many of us sought a simpler life. We wanted a Walden Pond, a place where the business of life could pass us by and answers could be found. Some attempted homesteading in Alaska, while others thought it might be found in communal living on the coasts of California or Oregon. But in the end, we discovered there were no utopias—and healthy answers couldn't be found though escapism. We learned that somehow the "peace" that was being preached had to be found within before it would ever manifest itself upon a world caught in crisis and chaos.

In 1971 Nancy and I took up residence on an isolated ranch that had been in my family for 70 years. The small cabin that became our home for the next 20 years was heated with an open fireplace and a wood burning stove in the small kitchen. Water was gravity fed from springs on the mountain, which was a wonderful convenience; however, we lived there for 14 years without electricity and for years without a phone. For all of those years, we were without television reception, relying only on books and each other for our entertainment. One Christmas to Nancy and our kids' great delight, I hooked up a strand of 12-volt lights to a car battery for the tree we had cut down on the mountain. We had a wonderful garden and orchard where we grew the majority of our food during our time there. Nancy canned and stored our reserves in a root cellar I had dug into the mountainside behind the cabin. Life in those days was quite simple and often filled with adventure that provided us all with fond memories to this day.

> Life in those days was quite simple and often filled with adventure that provided us all with fond memories to this day.

Although our physical life was isolated and basic, we quickly came to the reality that the complexity that robs one's peace doesn't solely come from a confusing world but rather from within. It was because of our desperation for truth and healing that in the solitude and simplicity of Robinson Canyon Ranch we discovered an authentic relationship with Christ. Our church community became not only a source of discipleship and spiritual grounding, but it provided meaningful and lasting relationships. Our early years were stretching in many ways, but the isolation of our lifestyle stimulated a season of growth and maturity both in our relationship with the Lord as well as with each other. Even our faith in God was without complexity. A simpler life gave us opportunity for a simple and pure devotion to Christ—and an opportunity to make a big impact on the lives of those around us.

A Timeless Problem

The idea that life can get beyond busy is nothing new. The apostle Paul warned the Christians in Corinth who were trying to grow amidst the confusion of their complex society: "… But I am afraid that, as the serpent deceived Eve by his craftiness, your minds will be led astray from the simplicity and purity of devotion to Christ." (2 Corinthians 11:3, NASB). In our culture today, it's challenging just to keep up with the Autobahn-like pace of the information super highway. We've seen a consistent revolution in the way we communicate from email to cell phones to text messaging. We broadcast ourselves on the Internet, share our stories on podcasts and blog about our daily life experiences. By the time this book finds its way to your hands, there will probably be another new form of innovative technology on the horizon that will again revolutionize the way we communicate and relate to one another. As our culture develops, there will always be good things to distract us from the most important things.

> We have almost emphatically declared as a society that we do too much, own too much, owe too much—all without doing much about it.

Before we go any further, we must define what simple living is. *Simple living* is a lifestyle that allows us to focus on the things that are most important to us, such as relationships both inside and outside of our families, without being encumbered by an inordinate amount of responsibilities that demand our attention. You can have few things but still have a complex life. People without much may conclude that having plenty of money will simplify their lives. People with an endless amount of assets and money may conclude that having less would be a much easier way to live. But the mistake we make in longing for a simplified life is that we believe it's only rooted in possessions. Real simple living does not leave any area of our lives untouched. Our time, our jobs, our finances, our hobbies, our possessions—they must all be assessed and reassessed on a regular basis to ensure that they are not stealing us away from those things that truly are most important.

As our culture grows more complex, there is a stirring within the west that maybe less is more. Has the great American dream become a living nightmare for too many of us? We have almost emphatically declared as a society that we do too much, own too much, owe too much—all without doing much about it. We must do more than just admit that a problem exists, a problem that is stealing away joy from our short, precious lives. But there are people who are beginning to do something about it. They are taking steps to render their lives down, enjoying more of what they have instead of trying to have more to enjoy. But is that the end game? To merely make a reduction in our lives?

Making a Smaller Footprint

One buzz phrase within environmental circles is "carbon footprint."[1] Companies and individuals that amass many possessions such as multiple houses, boats, cars, land, etc., are all leaving a big carbon footprint. The thing about a footprint is that it disturbs the peace of something in its environment—the bigger the footprint, the bigger the disturbance. Footprints sink deep into the ground without regard for the land on which they leave a lasting impression. It's merely a way to travel from one place to another. It's not creative; it's not thoughtful. It's nothing more than a big stamp of your presence that isn't positively memorable or helpful to others.

Likewise, we make a big footprint with the rest of our lives when we get involved in too many activities to really enjoy any of them or busily scurry about to make ends meet because we have too large of a mortgage payment or decide to acquire more possessions just because we want them. The wake of our lives is far-reaching, but more often than not, it's not in a positive way. We are seemingly everywhere, but truly present nowhere.

A smaller footprint can only occur when we make a concerted effort to live more simply. While I lived a simple life in nature on our family's ranch, things dramatically changed when I moved to Boise in 1989 to plant a church. Our work in Boise was both demanding and rewarding—and our lifestyle took a major turn. Planting a church takes everything you've got, especially in the first years of its conception. Our home became a center for church business, counseling and leadership training. My kids, Kate and Brook, were now in their teen years and enjoying a new life of social activity, athletics and outdoor recreation. For the first time we had a television in our home, a computer, and telephones that continually broke into our privacy with telemarketers interrupting our family dinner hour. It wasn't long before cell phones became a common part of the culture and email was the accepted form of daily communication. The promise that email would simplify communication quickly became a lie as it increased my work load. For the first time Nancy and I had a mortgage on our home and also entered into a partnership with a close friend on two rental houses for extra income. This required a fast learning curve due to my ignorance concerning such things as buying and selling properties, building codes and permits, escrows, interest rates, capital gains, 1031 exchanges and all the other pit falls of state and federal income and property taxes. Up until that point, we had only a simple checking and savings account, but suddenly we had to establish credit, take out home equity loans and periodically refinance for lower interest rates.

> We are seemingly everywhere, but truly present nowhere.

Because our kids were beginning to drive and own vehicles, and because we now owned properties, we not only had to increase our auto insurance but homeowners insurance and landlord insurance as well, not to mention title insurance and fire and flood insurance. Then there was health and dental insurance. With material ownership comes responsibility, so I took out life insurance for the first time, started a serious retirement savings plan, made out a will and eventually established a family trust with the help of a lawyer. It doesn't take long for life to get complicated, complex, and chaotic.

In addition to the demands of our personal life, I was now the senior pastor of a rapidly growing church that continued to require every bit of leadership ability I had to offer. Although most of what I have described is necessary in today's world, the simple life of solitude was gone and with it something precious had been lost. Our devotion to Christ and our love for his church hadn't diminished in any way, but the time to enjoy his presence was becoming an intentional discipline instead of a natural outflow of our lives.

By 2002 both of our kids were married and we had our first grandchild. We were dealing with the empty nest and characteristically were spoiling a new Golden Lab puppy. During this time, Nancy read from her Bible a passage that called us to "return to the things we did at first" and to remember what God had done for us in the beginning. (See Deuteronomy 4:9) It was then that the Lord miraculously opened the door for us to once again move to a quiet home in the hills about 50 minutes outside the city. Immediately, I took a short leave from church to spend about a month building fence lines, putting in an irrigation system and constructing a barn. Every morning I found myself sitting on the deck watching the first light of day cast its rays on a distant butte, feeling a cool morning breeze as I drank black coffee and embraced the lost luxury of unhindered silence. In those days something was restored in me, something was recaptured that I hadn't even realized had been lost.

Once I moved back to the mountains, spending time with the Lord became something I began to look forward to every morning and was no longer a scheduled discipline. I somehow returned to the thing I hadn't even realized had departed—and with it my zeal for life and creative juices began to flow in new and fresh ways. Nancy and I began to reevaluate how we were spending our time and reprioritized so that our energy would be expended on the things that were the most meaningful. New ideas for ministry began to emerge as God again had access to my thoughts and prayers. It was because of this new season of solitude that I decided to begin "Let's Tend the Garden," our church's environmental ministry, and a fast response disaster relief ministry that so effectively worked among the Hurricane Katrina victims in 2005.

In addition to ministry, the Lord began to speak to us about our personal lives as well. I began to feel a need to return to the joy of a simpler life, growing and raising our own food and becoming once again less dependent on the complexity of a technological world. I felt challenged to become more self-reliant when it came to energy, water and food sources. I knew from our previous life at the ranch how rewarding and invigorating it is to be more at home with the creation, and how refreshing it is to work hard with your hands doing purposeful creative work: "Begin using your hands for honest work, and then give generously to others in need" (Ephesians 4:28).

> Leaving a small footprint isn't about moving to the mountains or growing your own fruits and vegetables—it's about creating space in your life to do things that matter.

Now, before you close this book and dismiss this as pie-in-the-sky lifestyle dreaming, I know the logistics of my lifestyle are impractical for many people. In fact, it may not even be appealing to some of you reading this book. If you love living in an energy-driven urban area, living in the mountains may conjure up thoughts of a constricting, isolating way of life. Or you may want to live that way, but realize it's not going to happen in the near future as you're still in college or just starting a family. And that's fine. Leaving a small footprint isn't about moving to the mountains or growing your own fruits and vegetables—it's about creating space in your life to do things that matter.

As my personal footprint began to shrink, I began to notice a converse reaction, something that compelled me to teach about this within our congregation and share this principle with all who would listen. As a devoted follower of Jesus, I realized my decisions can't be based on good ideas but must be rooted in a biblical foundation that urges me to be more like Christ. And it's here that I realized that a small footprint alone is only half of the story. For when I begin to live simply thus leaving a smaller footprint, I can begin to love extravagantly thus making a bigger handprint. I can make a lasting positive impression, one through which my hands can be used to be the hands of Christ for a world desperate to see the love of Jesus demonstrated in a practical way.

Questions to Ponder:

1. How does your current lifestyle prohibit you from doing some of the things you most enjoy in life?

2. In what ways can you reduce the footprint of your life?

Small Footprint

Action Point: Keep a daily log of how you spend your time for an entire week and begin to rate what's most important to what's least important.

Looking Back

* Simple living is a lifestyle that allows us to focus on the things that are most important to us, such as relationships both inside and outside of our families, without being encumbered by an inordinate amount of responsibilities that demand our attention.

* A smaller footprint occurs when we make a concerted effort to live more simply.

* Leaving a small footprint isn't about moving to the mountains or growing your own fruits and vegetables—it's about creating space in your life to do things that matter.

chapter two

Big Handprint

Making a lasting positive impact

"I want real relationships – I know a lot of people. I want freedom – not freedom to do what I want, but freedom to sleep well at night without worry. I want to devote my life to something that lasts longer than I do."
—Mark Tabb, Living on Less

Let God transform you into a new person by changing the way you think. Then you will know what God wants you to do, and you will know how good and pleasing and perfect his will really is.
– Romans 12:2

Meet my friend, Eric, a young man whose story is similar to that of a growing number in our church community. Eric understood what it meant to have a small footprint; it was just making a difference with his life that seemed out of his grasp. Armed with a GED and some handyman skills, he heard the call to make a big handprint while watching a Purpose Driven Life simulcast with Rick Warren in our church one Sunday—and he answered it.

"Rick Warren talked about how his dad had just a fishing pole, a tool bag and his Bible, and how God had used his dad all over the world to build churches and show other people God's love in a practical way," Eric recalls. "So, I thought, 'What could I bring to the table?' I was a builder, but I had no idea what else that would look like. I just wanted to do something."

Unencumbered by debt or other obligations, Eric had only to convince his wife, Linsey, to embark on this journey together. Just six months into their marriage, Linsey agreed and they took their first step into making a lasting impact. They attended a missions school in the Philippines, unsure of what might become of their adventure. Both were trained in primary healthcare, and Eric eventually went on a short tour with a dentist, pulling teeth of people living in impoverished areas of the Philippines.

After his time there ended, Eric took two weeks to find out if pulling teeth was really something he wanted to do as part of his missions work in the future. He flew into a dangerous area of the Philippines to meet a dentist for another short tour. During his stay there, Eric rode dirt bikes with this dentist into the jungle of remote villages to pull teeth, even getting an armed escort by government soldiers to protect them from guerrillas at one juncture.

"Pulling teeth was one of the most gratifying and fulfilling things I've ever done," says Eric, who had dropped out of high school and became entrenched in the marijuana drug culture before later accepting Christ. "Some of these people had had aching teeth for a year and could barely eat. To pull their teeth one day and see them smiling from ear to ear with a mouthful of gauze the next was an amazing experience. ... The Philippines is a place overflowing with religions and missionaries from cults and other religions—and all those different religions demand things from the people. It was nice just to go into their communities and villages and show them God's love in a very practical way with no expectations for anything."

"Most of my life up until that point had been doing everything for myself everyday. But I wanted to do something more, something that mattered. In some cases, the people there have free healthcare from the government, but it's not really the best care. I want to give these people what they deserve, which is great healthcare and from someone who cares about them as a person, too."

For others, it's a haunting reminder years later of how much time they have let slip away in pursuit of the mundane over the meaningful.

Eric and Linsey remained in the Philippines for an additional 18 months helping with various mission agencies and local churches before making the decision to return home. But instead of going back to his status quo life, Eric enrolled in college to begin working toward medical school with an eye on returning one day in some capacity.

"We're not sure what it will look like at this point," says Eric, who still uses his handyman skills to help pay the bills while going to school. "But we know that we want to help people in some way and we can do that through the healthcare profession."

When the window of the world is flung open to young people, many of them declare that their lives will be about changing the world. And for a handful, that declaration is a precursor to action. For others, it's merely a haunting reminder years later of how much time they have let slip away in pursuit of the mundane over the meaningful. But no matter where we are in our life's journey, we can always readjust our vision and begin seeing the world around us through the lens of an eternal perspective.

True simplicity begins when we come to grips with the real nature of the universe, understanding that it will keep running well beyond our last breath. And true followers of Jesus recognize that a Kingdom perspective happens with one eye on eternity at all times. Is what you're doing today going to matter tomorrow? Are the choices you are making now mindful of the future? God's redemptive plan for humanity and creation doesn't begin in some distant future—it has already begun. We won't see the fullness of it for quite some time, but whenever we experience God's presence in our lives, pushing us closer to him as we reach out to others, we see glimpses of God's Kingdom in the here and now.

Leaving a big handprint occurs when we make ourselves available to be used by God for his plans and purposes. It speaks of the extent to which the love of God flows through our lives into the lives of others. The apostle Paul writes, "Don't copy the behavior and customs of this world, but let God transform you into a new person by changing the way you think. Then you will know what God wants you to do, and you will know how good and pleasing and perfect his will really is" (Romans 12:2). When God changes the way we think, he reverses the ideals valued by our culture that don't align with his Word—ideals like the more you have, the happier you'll be. The reason many people spend their entire lives longing to make a difference in this world but never doing so is because they haven't allowed God to transform the way they think.

> The reason many people spend their entire lives longing to make a difference in this world but never doing so is because they haven't allowed God to transform the way they think.

Oftentimes, our shortsightedness prevents us from recognizing God's plans and purposes for our lives. We become so myopic that all we see is today or maybe a week from today. There is no eye on eternity; there is no contemplation of the impact our actions will have on the future and future generations. In addressing the future of Christianity at a gathering of leaders, *Wired* magazine executive editor Kevin Kelly explained that due to life expectancy and other trends, futurists are predicting humanity is only 13 generations away from the next 1,000 years.[1] That tells us what we do today can have enormous influence over the future of faith in the world. Our handprint can be bigger than we ever imagined when put into the context of that prediction.

Jesus' Big Handprint

Getting out a message in our culture today is challenging. You must compete with advertising giants who know how to work the system to influence people and bring about cultural change. And it seems that if God really wanted to have a maximum impact on reaching humanity, he would've chosen to send Jesus to earth in an era where it was easier to spread his message of love, forgiveness, peace and redemption. But he didn't. God chose to spread his message through his son made flesh as a carpenter. Not just any carpenter, but one from Nazareth—a town that was not highly regarded by society. And he did it in an era devoid of all the modern tools we have for communicating to mass amounts of people.

Instead of a big media campaign, Jesus' platform developed through a consistent message of love and peace, healing and forgiveness. People flocked to hear him speak and witness the miracles he performed. His disciples grew under his tutelage and eventually became the pillars of the early church. Jesus' handprint on 12 men continues to leave its mark on the earth to this day—and will do so for years to come.

In calling people into a loving relationship with God, Jesus explained that the simplicity of doing his works enable us to disencumber ourselves from the things that keep us from leaving a big handprint on those around us. It's as if we have to battle ourselves at times to shirk our idea of self-importance. Jesus did not call us to prop ourselves up; he called us to prop up others, serving them with love and caring for them due to the sheer fact that it's God's heart to do so. Consider this passage from The Message:

> Meanwhile the tax man, slumped in the shadows, his face in his hands, not daring to look up, said, "God, give mercy. Forgive me, a sinner." Jesus commented, "This tax man, not the other, went home made right with God. If you walk around with your nose in the air, you're going to end up flat on your face, but if you're content to be simply yourself, you will become more than yourself."
>
> – Luke 18:13-14

In God's simplistic design, he made each one of us capable of doing the work that he has called us to do. He gave us Jesus as a model and the Holy Spirit as a helper. And we're called to be a reflection of Jesus, leaving behind a handprint on this world as well. *God's heart for stewardship is not that we would waste our lives here on earth and bide our time until we get to heaven, but rather that we would pursue with abandonment the call to love him and others, caring for the things that are important to him.*

Quest for Significance

As we watch the time we have on earth slip away, almost everyone has an experience where they wake up and realize that they are tired of living the way they are living. They want their lives to be significant, full of meaning and purpose. They want to be able to answer this question affirmatively: "Will the world know that I was here?" And the pathway for that to occur in our lives begins when we understand the three most important events in our human experience.

1. Discover the Creator for yourself. There's a big difference between being told all about a person and actually meeting him or her. Stories only capture glimpses of the person's character and nature and presence. But experiencing those stories with the person changes everything. Your story is now intertwined with that person's story, forever linked together. People can tell us all about God, but until we experience his amazing love and grace and forgiveness for ourselves, it's just another good story, becoming even unfathomable at times. Once we discover the Creator and experience him for ourselves, our path toward significance will begin to accelerate.

> Once we discover God and figure out his purpose for our lives, it's time to take action.

2. Discover why you were created. In finding significance, we must understand that there is a purpose for each of our lives. The scope of influence and impact may vary from person to person, but everyone has purpose. There are volumes and volumes of books that are willing to guide you through that process. However, it begins with a simple acknowledgement that God does have big plans for our lives and that he will show them to us if we ask him.

3. Do what you were created to do for the rest of your life. There are no accidents with God—and we will never live the adventure he has for us if we think our life is insignificant. Once we discover God and figure out his purpose for our lives, it's time to take action. It's time to start leaving a big handprint.

If you don't believe that God has a special purpose for you, consider the words of the apostle Paul:

> In his grace, God has given us different gifts for doing certain things well. So if God has given you the ability to prophesy, speak out with as much faith as God has given you. If your gift is

serving others, serve them well. If you are a teacher, teach well. If your gift is to encourage others, be encouraging. If it is giving, give generously. If God has given you leadership ability, take the responsibility seriously. And if you have a gift for showing kindness to others, do it gladly.

– Romans 12:6-8

Paul goes on to say in verse 12 that we should "be glad for all God is planning for you." In other words, whatever God sets before you, do it with passion and fervor—and know that these are his plans for you.

Answering the Call

At our church, we have created a culture among our leaders of inviting people to engage in ministry, oftentimes stretching people beyond their comfort zones. One of our pastors, Tim McFarlane, saw something brewing in a Vietnam veteran in our church named Ken Moore—and he invited Ken to accompany us on a trip to Zambia to dig fresh water wells. What God is doing in his life as a result is truly amazing, but God was at work in Ken long before any invitation was issued.

Ken grew up on a ranch in Nevada, living in a culture that resisted the idea that you ever needed anyone else's help. As a "functional" drunk at the age of 50, he decided that way of living was foolish—especially if he wanted to be sober. He joined Alcoholic Anonymous and discovered Christ in the process, learning for the first time what it meant to truly follow Jesus despite regularly attending church as a child. When Ken, who worked as a finishing carpenter, began meeting people while working on a construction project at our church, he decided to start attending.

For the past 12 years, Ken has remained sober with the help and encouragement of a community of believers. But God had more for

Ken than simply being sober—he was preparing to harvest seeds that had been planted in Ken years before during one of his tours in Vietnam.

"At one point in Vietnam, I was in a recon platoon in a mountain infantry," Ken says. "We were living in these villages where special forces had armed the people living there. And I really became attached to the people. After the war was over, I had a thought about helping people like them, but nothing really came of it until about 40 years later."

At age 62, Ken responded to those seeds planted in him and struck off halfway around the world with us to Zambia. In the process, he discovered that sharing the Gospel is sometimes as easy as picking up a hammer. "While we were there, I did a lot of the physical stuff," Ken says. "I'm not a preacher by any means, but I thought I'd like to help the people there. It was really a neat experience for me.

"It wasn't anything like I thought it would be. There was a real hopeless poverty among these people. The people we were helping really needed help in the worst way. And we weren't a bunch of people on a holiday looking to make ourselves feel better—there was a purpose for being there. But we didn't want to go over there and take our ideas and way of doing things to them; we just wanted to go over there and help them. We didn't have any type of miraculous encounter with God, but you could feel God with us."

This experience forever ruined Ken, who returned a few months later with his wife to oversee new construction projects in Zambia for a month. Status quo life in Idaho just won't do it for him anymore. That's what we can all expect when we respond to the call God places in front of us with obedience. Ken may not have thought he had much to offer, but he did—he had himself to offer. And the impact of his willingness to do so has left a lasting impression, a large handprint, on a community in Zambia ... and on his own life.

Hand in Hand

Leaving a small footprint and a big handprint can seem daunting at times. But this is a symbiotic relationship. To truly leave the kind of handprint that God has destined for us to leave on this world, we must be careful where we tread. Our impact can be softened when these two elements are not carefully weighed and measured. We can be a great force in our communities for good, but if we're not sensitive to the culture in which we live, we can all but cancel out good works. Jesus didn't counteract his miracles by offending people (with the exception of religious types who needed to have their sensibilities offended to be shaken out of their pious stupor). Instead, his handprint was expanded because of the way he extravagantly loved people. The outcast, the sick, the poor, the children—all of them were welcome in his presence. Those who complained were quickly rebuked and reminded that this type of love and acceptance marked by serving the people society has marginalized was the heart of his message. Jesus wanted everyone to know that every person is important, that they all have a place at his Father's table in Heaven. And it was a message delivered with all the love and compassion consistent with leaving a small footprint.

> Or do we want to be known as followers of Jesus whose hands were worn and dirty from serving and loving everyone in our world, regardless of who they were or what they believed?

Do we want to be known as followers of Jesus who trampled the world around us with our theology and ideals? Or do we want to be known as followers of Jesus whose hands were worn and dirty from serving and loving everyone in our world, regardless of who they were or what they believed?

Even entire churches have seen the need for this type of transformation in their approach to ministering to their community. One pastor friend of mine discovered the reality of how empty church and the

Christian faith can be when it's detached from making a big impact. Living in the New Orleans area, he awoke one morning in the aftermath of the Hurricane Katrina disaster to a stark truth about his church: they were attracting people based on what it had to offer its people as opposed to what its people had to offer the community around it. The question he challenged himself and the rest of the church with was this: "Other than wrapping Christmas presents for free for people at the mall once a year, would people notice if our church disappeared? Would the community miss us at all?" In other words, if we suddenly moved out or shut down, would our handprint leave a lasting impressions on the lives of those in our community or would our legacy be an empty building that eventually becomes an eye sore?

This is precisely the reason why many people in our culture want nothing to do with church—many churches aren't doing anything except facilitating an organization akin to a bridge club or a service organization. Sure, it's a fun place to hang out and meet people, but its purpose has become lost amidst a sea of church marketing and the desire to be cool. Sure, you might even have an opportunity to serve your community, but it's lost among a current of other do-gooders. If we want our lives to count for something, we must leave a handprint that points people to the heart of Christ. If we want our churches to be "cool," let's love the unlovable and serve people in ways no one else is serving them. If we want to—as St. Francis of Assisi put it—"kiss the leper's hand," we need to resist culture's norm to serve ourselves and learn how to serve others in meaningful ways that transform their lives.

In order to sustain this way of living, however, we must create room in our lives to do it. So, let's explore together how to keep this intricate balance of small footprint and big handprint in check—and change our world in the most exciting adventure we'll ever embark upon.

Questions to Ponder:

1. How are you currently impacting the world in which you live?

2. In what ways can you increase the handprint of your life?

Big Handprint

Action Point: Write down one area you would like to make a difference in the world whether it be with young people, seniors, kids, rich, poor, helpless, confused, etc. Find an organization in your community that can help make that idea a reality and volunteer.

Looking Back

* Leaving a big handprint occurs when we make ourselves available to be used by God for his plans and purposes.

* The reason many people spend their entire lives longing to make a difference in this world but never doing so is because they haven't allowed God to transform the way they think.

* Once you discover God and the purpose He has for you, it's time to take action.

chapter three

Pathway to Adventure

Seizing opportunity at every turn

*"It is the responsibility of leadership to
provide opportunity, and the responsibility of
individuals to contribute."*
– C. William Pollard,
chairman of the ServiceMaster Company

*"Anyone who puts a hand to the plow and then looks
back is not fit for the Kingdom of God."*
– Luke 9:62

When I was in junior high, I came across my dad's old scrapbook, which documented the adventures of his youth. His experiences were so thrilling I almost needed the scrapbook to believe they were entirely true. Even in my wildest imagination, I struggled to conceive of the things he did all over the country.

He rode his bicycle from Long Beach, Calif., to Michigan—not once, but twice—pedaling on many dirt roads in the process. One time he decided to visit one of the most remote locations in the U.S., which he determined to be a settlement with no roads leading in or out in the Escalante River area in Utah. He rode his bike as far as he could go before getting lost in the river drainages—and the way he survived was by killing a deer with his rifle and turning the meat into venison jerky. He eventually stumbled across a sheepherder who fed him for a while. Then he caught a wild horse, broke it and rode it into this remote community where he milked cows for a summer to earn enough money to buy another horse. He left the community with two horses.

Then he sailed a 16-foot sailboat from Seattle to Alaska, getting shipwrecked once before safely arriving, where he washed dishes to put himself through school at the University of Alaska-Fairbanks. Later, he earned one of the first pilots' licenses issued in the Yukon Territory, and eventually became a bush pilot before returning to the continental U.S. and serving as a fighter pilot in World War II.

Whenever I read his scrapbook, I said in awe, "Now that is adventure" and attempted to model my life that way, unaware of the fact that my dad put these adventures into the context of understanding what it meant to follow Jesus. Nevertheless, I rode my bike up and down U.S. Highway 1. I earned my pilots' license on the day I turned 17 and flew all over the backcountry of Idaho in the 1960s. I sky dived, mountain climbed, anything for a thrill and a rush. But in the midst of all that pursuit of adventure, I never had a real sense of fulfillment. During that time, I failed to understand that I could only find real adventure in the Kingdom of God.

Reflecting on my life as a passionate follower of Jesus, I now realize what an adventure I've had since committing my life to him. I've hiked through the backcountry of Burma on mission expeditions, preached in villages to the Karen people on the border of Thailand and Burma, smuggled Bibles into China right after Mao Tse Tung's death when the border was opened, went through the Amazon River basin on a riverboat planting churches. My adventure didn't exist solely on the completion of life-threatening tasks; I once taught a Filipino woman how to pack a horse so she could carry medical supplies into remote mountain villages. That experience was just as thrilling and adventurous for me as anything else I had done—I was serving Christ in that moment by loving and serving this woman in a practical way.

Today, we live in a world full of artificial adventure. We push the envelope more and more to try to get a bigger adrenaline rush and do something more outrageous than before. And for many, the drive to do something adrenaline-pumping grows stronger because these false adventures are increasingly unfulfilling. At each turn, adventure seekers are forced to look in the mirror and wonder why they must continue to push the limits—and why what they do never fully satisfies them. When it comes to adventure, there's nothing artificial about living a life of radical faith; however, we don't choose our adventure—it chooses us.

In our desire to love extravagantly and leave behind a large handprint full of the markings of Christ's love, we must remember that adventure with God begins with simplicity. You can't go on a treacherous hike with 200 pounds of gear strapped to your back and you certainly can't embark on God's adventure for your life with other things weighing you down. Addictions, habitual sin, and being owned by our stuff are all heavy elements that will complicate our lives and render our adventures either extremely laborious or non-existent.

Radical faith is best expressed when we're living simply, unencumbered by the things of this world.

Living the Adventure

The word "advent" literally means *a momentous arrival*. When we celebrate advent at Christmas, we're doing just that—celebrating the momentous arrival of Jesus on the earth. Today, we're living at a place in history between the first and second advent of Christ. And it's what we do with our time now that will determine to what extent we spread Christ's love by practically demonstrating his care and concern for humanity and teaching people about a pathway to forgiveness and redemption.

Our adventure begins when we start proclaiming and demonstrating the message of the Kingdom of God. Some churches choose to ignore or minimize the demonstration of the message, stating that they don't want to develop a social Gospel. But there is only one Gospel, which is a proclamation of the Good News through both our mouths and our actions. As the church, we cannot simply behave as a charity, sweeping under the rug our motivation for serving others. Nor can we simply talk about the Gospel without doing anything about it. Daring faith does both, getting dirty when necessary through serving others and speaking the truth when the time calls for it.

> Today, we're living at a place in history between the first and second advent of Christ.

Now more than ever, people who profess to be followers of Jesus must resist casual Christianity in lieu of coming to the aid of a world in decline. Everywhere we look, there are images of a suffering humanity just begging for the practical demonstrations of the Gospel. Digging wells in Africa, caring for those infected with HIV, rescuing those trapped in sex slave trade, building houses in the Gulf Coast region—this is the heart of God. Without a doubt, these are some of

> How poised the church is to experience a real reformation by coming to the aid of a dying world that feels hopelessly trapped in a never-ending cycle of poverty and sickness.

the issues Jesus would have addressed if he lived during our lifetime.

How poised the church is to experience a real reformation by coming to the aid of a dying world that feels hopelessly trapped in a never-ending cycle of poverty and sickness. The world needs to experience a practical demonstration of the Gospel in order to realize that there is a God in Heaven who not only knows each person's name but also knows each person's pain. God's love for us runs so deep that he uses broken people who have discovered his empowering love to demonstrate love to those in dire need of assurance that God is still there—and that he cares.

From Opportunity to Crisis to Opportunity

Ironically enough, it's the land of opportunity and some of its twisted values that have created a global crisis. The American lifestyle has been nurtured and even glamorized by its dependency on oil. As the greatest consumer of energy and fossil fuels, the U.S. has moved full speed ahead, ignoring the consequences of what such a lifestyle might eventually bring to future generations. With the rise of capitalism in China and the surge of economic growth in India, the U.S. is no longer alone at top of the energy supply chain. Now the U.S. must contend with China and India for such energy resources. If nothing is done to correct this problem (part of which could be helped by simpler living in the U.S.), the perfect storm just might be brewing.

Then there's climate change. While scientists and political leaders are embroiled in a battle over what is causing it, nations are shifting. Sea levels are rising, glaciers are melting, and farmers are being forced to grow crops no longer viable in certain changing climates. Due to its severe poverty, Bangladesh can't afford the type of preventative measures being used in low-lying areas throughout Europe and in New Orleans. "It is poor countries that are suffering the brunt of climate change," Saleemul Huq, the climate change program director for the International Institute for Environment and Development, told *Time* magazine. "But it is the rich countries' greenhouse gas emissions that caused this problem in the first place."

There is also a widening gap between the rich and the poor. And while this may not alarm many staunch capitalists, its catastrophic consequences should send off warning signals to followers of Jesus: Out of this desperation of poverty, human slave trafficking is on the rise. The value of a human is becoming less and less. The U.S. State Department estimates between 600,000 and 800,000 people are trafficked across international borders for various reasons, including sex trade and child soldiers.[1] Coming full circle on this issue, some of the children in villages without fresh water wells are captured and forced into the sex slave trade market while walking to get water.

> Christians in the West must have their hearts broken over issues such as these and must begin to pay attention to these worldwide epidemics instead of dismissing them as someone else's problem.

Christians in the western world must have their hearts broken over issues such as these and must begin to pay attention to these worldwide epidemics instead of dismissing them as someone else's problem. What is considered the "American dream" has become a nightmare for many here, not to mention millions around the world. And as Christians who have the means to act, what will we do? Will we sit idly by and just hope the storm will pass? Or will we be proactive, practically demonstrating the love of Christ to people impoverished monetarily and spiritually? As a follower of Jesus, status quo life is no good anymore—it just doesn't seem right. We must put ourselves in a position to be more effective with the life we have left. And that means starting with downsizing

and simplifying our lives into a more basic way—the way we started—
so that we're more free to   proclaim and demonstrate the Gospel
around the world to people in crisis.

When followers of Jesus begin to take this charge seriously, we will
see a different kind of reformation in the church, the kind of reformation that forever ruins us for church the way it is today. I'm a firm
believer that the local church is what brings hope to the world
through practical demonstrations of the Gospel. And if the church is
willing to cast off "the way we've always done things" and revisit what
God says about the way He intended for us to live life and serve those
around us, we will see a reformation that so many people—young and
old—are clamoring for.

The adventure is not an organization; it's a philosophy. We can't
capture it into a program and market it to those in our community.
The adventure is simply embracing the idea that
we can join a movement that is a spirit-inspired
and change people's lives. Try as we may, we
can't keep God under control. It's up to us to
recognize what he is doing and join him in the
great adventure that he is laying out for all his
people who will willfully and joyfully follow.

> The adventure
> is simply
> embracing the
> idea that we
> can join a
> movement that
> is a spirit-
> inspired and
> change people's
> lives.

However, in order for any of us to embrace
the adventure fully, we have to travel light.
There is little room for complexity when we are
consumed with sharing the simple message of
God's love for others. When God calls us, we
must be ready to drop everything in our heavy load. Consider Jesus'
exchange with two people he asked to follow him:

> He said to another person, "Come, be my disciple." The man
> agreed, but he said, "Lord, first let me return home and bury my
> father." Jesus replied, "Let those who are spiritually dead care for
> their own dead. Your duty is to go and preach the coming of the

Kingdom of God." Another said, "Yes, Lord, I will follow you, but first let me say good-bye to my family." But Jesus told him, "Anyone who puts a hand to the plow and then looks back is not fit for the Kingdom of God."

– Luke 9:59-62

I want to be fit for the Kingdom of God. Whenever God calls me to do something, I want to be able to do it immediately, free from excessive responsibility that prohibits me from following him fully. And when I'm living a simplified life, I'm more free to love others, demonstrating the power of the Gospel at its essence.

A Series of Small Decisions

Because of our growing passion for environmental stewardship, I began to establish numbers of new relationships with Christian leaders across the country who were working throughout the developing world on various environmental projects. People like Scott Sabin, the leader of Floresta, an organization that focuses on reforestation in places like Haiti, and Kirk Shower, the founder of Seeds of Hope, which is providing fresh drinkable water for the poor by means of filtering and well drilling in Africa.[2] Through speaking with these leaders we began to realize just how much our declining global environment has been directly affecting the poor, causing entire groups of people to suffer. We have met an amazing new network of creative people who are connecting the ministry of Jesus to world crises. Some are working in the area of health care, some in agriculture, some in human trafficking, and others in skill training and education. At some point in time all of these people got in touch with the heart of God concerning the fulfilled ministry of Isaiah 61 and made a choice to do what they could for the poor, the brokenhearted, and the captive. All of them had come to the conclusion that having a theology for the ministry wasn't enough—they had to act on it. For some of them it meant huge lifestyle commitments, but for others it was just a matter of awareness and the decision to make small changes.

While returning from a trip to a very poor district on the border of Zambia and the Congo, Nancy and I were making the endless flight from Africa back to the States. During that flight we both watched the movie *Blood Diamond*. I had put off seeing this movie because I knew about its graphic nature and devastating plot, but knowing it dealt with the humanity crises in the area we had just visited, we both decided to use the time we had to view it. You may know that the movie deals directly with the very current, very real problem of human slave trade and child soldiering, which is fueled by the black market diamond trade.

If you haven't seen it, I warn you it is eye opening and devastating. The movie accurately portrays a very real problem, and combined with the fact that we had just been among the very people who were so vulnerable to these atrocities, it deeply impacted us both. As the movie ended neither of us spoke for a long time. We sat in the darkness, fighting the tears that began welling up. Our hearts had been broken and feelings of overwhelming hopelessness began to grip us. The problem was too big and too horrendous. What could we do to make a difference against such an atrocity? It was all too out of control and too impossible. Breaking the silence Nancy turned to me and said, "I never want you to buy me another diamond." She was simply stating that she had to do something and this was all she knew to do. She was saying that she didn't care if this was merely one grain of sand on an endless beach—at least it was something. If her desire to own a diamond was in anyway contributing to the world's demand for diamonds then it simply wasn't worth it. Sometimes a small footprint is a simple action based on a

> The Christian life is a life of activism based on biblical principal, and if we don't respond to the brokenness of the world in some way, nothing will ever change.

righteous conviction. Too often Americans are exposed to the atrocities of a broken world and do nothing in their belief that their life is too insignificant or that the problem is too far removed from their suburban life. The Christian life is a life of activism based on biblical principal, and if we don't respond to the brokenness of the world in some way, nothing will ever change. Small footprints generally require small actions—and it's those small actions that oftentimes lead us into the adventure of a lifetime.

Questions to Ponder

1. In what ways have you experienced adventure in your life?

2. What opportunities do you have to put this definition of adventure into action?

Small Footprint

Action point: Make a list of some luxury items you've purchased in the past two years and select one that you could do without or don't use nearly as much as you thought you would. Sell it and ...

Big Footprint

Action Point: ... find an organization that strikes a chord with some social issue that's important to you and donate the money from the sale of your luxury item to that group.

Looking Back

* Our adventure begins when we start proclaiming and demonstrating the message of the Kingdom of God.

* A practical demonstration of the Gospel is what the world needs to experience in order to realize that there is a God in Heaven who not only knows each person's name but also knows each person's pain.

* The adventure is simply embracing the idea that we can join a movement that is a spirit-inspired and changing people's lives.

chapter four

A Simple Solution

The answer to two
daunting commissions

"Whoso loves, believes the impossible."
— Elizabeth Barrett Browning

And as soon as they landed, they left everything
and followed Jesus.
— Luke 5:11

If you want to see teenagers get excited about something, explain to them the rules of "Bigger is Better" and turn them loose. The game begins with each team receiving a small item, such as a paper clip. They have to trade that item for something bigger and bring back their biggest object at a designated deadline. The idea is to keep trading up and hope your aren't outdone by the competing teams. At the final "weigh-in", some teams will come back with washing machines, trucks or even fire engines.

It feels like many adults are engaged in a life-long game of "Bigger is Better." Some people's favorite word is "upgrade." Their unquenchable desire for more is destructive not only to the earth's physical environment but also to their hearts' emotional environments.

In one fell swoop, a person who puts all their energy into this type of "bigger is better" life pursuit leaves an ugly wake. So, they have the biggest house on the street. In most cases, these external monuments have dire consequences for our environment in the amount of energy it takes to keep them. Already, their footprint is anything but small. Likewise, this type of life pursuit leaves a person little time to actually do something that matters on this earth. And no matter how big your house is, when your time here is up, the house isn't going with you. Those people are left pondering this question for eternity, "Why did I waste my time pursuing meaningless things?" I certainly do not want to be one of those people. As my friend Ed McGlasson likes to ask, "Why settle for a monument when you can be part of a movement that changes the world?"

These lavish consumer lifestyles are glamorized by our culture and viewed as the symbol of success. Sadly, these big footprints are destroying creation as well as people's livelihoods. Our planet is fragile and delicately woven together by the Creator, yet people have ignored the warning signs of our hurting planet in favor of creating more goods that find a fast track to overflowing our landfills, yet leave people empty inside. Corporate greed has seeped into most western-ers' consumer mentality. While many activists shake an angry fist at corporations, consumers are just as guilty, succumbing to the idea that we need the latest gizmo or gadget to make our lives happy.

During the summer of 2007, there was a developing story that occupied my thoughts and made me ponder the possible dire out-come. Scientists and researchers began noticing a sharp decline in the number of honey bee colonies throughout North America and Europe. By the end of the summer, some scientists estimated 50 per-cent of the colonies had disappeared, many without so much as a sign or warning. One of the theories that flowed forth horrified me when I began to follow the consequences through in my mind—cell phones. Some researchers initially offered a theory that cell phone radiation could be the culprit. And I wondered, *Would the world give up this relatively new technology to save bees? Do people even realize the value of honey bees? Would people sacrifice their current way of life for the planet and ultimately for future generations?* In the end, scientists discovered the cause was a virus, yet I couldn't shake the idea from my head that people would probably be unwilling to change their lifestyles to save bees. Many people would scoff at the idea, even if it were proven true. I'm guessing most people would balk at the notion of giving up their cell phones, unable to realize the importance of bees in our ecosystem and the vast impact their disappearance would have on the earth.

However, there are places where this idea of changing one's lifestyle for the sake of the planet is actually being forced upon peo-ple—and it's a fight. The state of Georgia has been experiencing a drought for a number of years now and the water table in the lakes and reservoirs surrounding Atlanta has slowly dropped as the popula-tion has swelled to over five million. In the summer of 2007, water-ing bans were enforced but ignored by many. One local TV station aired a story about a house that consumed an average of 400,000 gal-lons of water per month. (By comparison, the American Water Works

Association estimates that the average American household uses 10,500 gallons per month.) Despite the drought and new rate hikes on massive residential consumers, nothing at this house was changing or will likely change anytime soon.

Changing our lifestyle is admittedly difficult, especially after we have grown comfortable and accustomed to our current one. But we must realize that lifestyle changes must occur in order for us to reduce our footprint and increases our capacity to love others and leave a big handprint.

> We must realize that lifestyle changes must occur in order for us to reduce our footprint and increases our capacity to love others and leave a big handprint.

When you become a follower of Christ, you discover that there is a new way to live. You define success differently. You welcome the new-found freedom in your life and wonder how you ever lived any other way. You also learn of two important commissions Jesus gave us:

1. **Care for creation.** This is done in the same way you would govern a people—you take care of and protect them. (See Genesis 1:28)

2. **Make disciples.** This doesn't mean you have them repeat a short prayer and you're done. Disciples do what their teacher does. So, the process of discipleship is an involved one. (See Matthew 28:19)

You also learn that there's one command that teaches us how to fulfill both commissions. But more on that later.

Our First Commission: Care for Creation

In my book, *Saving God's Green Earth*, I focused on the importance of this commission, why the church has abandoned it and what it can do to regain this once-beloved value and become leaders in the charge to save the world. Whenever you start breaking status quo, look out. I was reminded of that fact quite often as I attempted to have rational discussions with fellow believers. Many people in the western world have a hard time seeing beyond the politics of caring for the environment, unwilling to work with someone they view as a political enemy even when it's to their detriment.[1] For me, the bigger issue is this: Are we being obedient to what God has called us to do as his people?

In Genesis 1:28, God makes it clear that we are to have dominion over nature. Sadly, many people have misinterpreted this verse as "do whatever you want to do with it." Any person attuned to God's heart for his creation would quickly realize the inaccuracies of that interpretation. God gives us the ability to make our own choices, but his hope is that we choose his way over meaningless, empty and destructive paths. He cares about us and he cares about his creation.

Consider the story of Noah for just a moment. If you have time (and you should have more now that you're simplifying your life, right?), read Noah's story in Genesis 6-9. What you'll find are five major points to this story when it comes to understanding God's first commission for us to care for the earth.

1. Revelation. We first have to come to the reality that God exists. Noah not only believed God existed but he "walked with God" (Genesis 6:9). Therefore, Noah was following God, listening to his voice and obeying his commands.

2. Obedience. If we believe God exists and we believe his way is best, we need to begin following his directions for our lives. Noah does this as God gives him various tasks and assignments in preparation for the flood: "And Noah did all that the Lord commanded him" (Genesis 7:5).

3. Redemption. In this story, God obviously allowed people and animals to perish—but he didn't destroy all that he had created. In fact, his heart was to save all that he could. What ended up being saved? Faithful man and God's creation.

4. Responsibility and Dominion. After the waters receded, God made a covenant with man and his creation. But he also gave Noah and his sons directions on how to walk out this covenant, highlighting important elements. God called them to have dominion over his creation (Genesis 9:2), showed them how his creation served as provision (v. 3), demanded responsibility and accountability (v. 5), explained the sanctity of human life (v. 6), and called for multiplication and inhabiting of the earth (v. 7).

5. God's Covenant, Promise and Commission. God made a serious covenant, one that we shouldn't take lightly. It was lasting (Genesis 9:9), visible (v. 13), and applicable to man, plants and animals (v. 10). In fact, God so emphasized how this covenant was between him and all his creation that he saw the need to state it six times in Genesis 9.

When we read this story in its entirety, we discover that this is a commission for us to care for the earth—and the practical way we do this is through a small footprint. In our culture today, it demands it. We need to become better stewards of this beautiful earth God has given us.

Our Second Commission: Make Disciples

When we planted the church in Boise, my vision was to develop a group of passionate followers of Christ who would change the world. Through their deep devotion to Jesus, they would experience immeasurable changes in their lives through character development and daily commitment to walk out their faith. In today's day and age of "Bigger is Better" church growth emphasis, this idea either sounds foreign or too idealistic. But I knew this was the direction God had for our church.

Now, don't get me wrong: When it comes to church growth, I'm not afraid of becoming a big church. And with the way our church has grown, I'm getting more comfortable with the idea. But whether your church is 50 or 10,000, the commission of making disciples needs to be fulfilled. It's the parting words of Jesus—and we need to take those words to heart.

Seven years after we planted the church, attendance was surging at such a pace that created challenges for our staff to keep with the growth. The worship was passionate. People seemed to enjoy coming to church. But I recognized a problem that wasn't easily detectable upon glancing at the congregation on Sunday mornings. I heard the stories and saw the consequences of lives that weren't being changed. Our church looked great, but the top mission wasn't being fulfilled. A dynamic church that is making disciples understands that what happens Mondays through Saturdays is just as important as what happens on Sundays. We were failing miserably at this task.

After complaining about this problem to the Lord for a while, I prayed about it and felt like he inspired me with some structural ideas that would help facilitate this mission. (I wrote more about this in my book *Revolutionary Leadership*.) I tore down our existing leadership structure and started from scratch, asking every leader to go through our new structural system. Only one couple refused before eventually relenting and complying. What followed was an amazing shift in the culture of our church. We began to fulfill our top mission by making disciples. This still continues to this day where each week we have a segment of our Sunday morning service where we watch a video about a member of our church or a group of people in our church who are doing something to change the world. Whether it's leading a friend to Christ, going on a mission trip, serving the poor or helping refugees, our church sees that discipleship is a verb. Discipleship isn't about what you say you believe; it's about what you *demonstrate* you believe.

In Luke 5, Jesus gathers a handful of his disciples. But he doesn't have tryouts or sift through applications. He simply says, "This is who

I am. This is where I'm going. Are you with me?" Much like the commission to care for creation, Jesus lays out many of the same principles in calling Peter, James and John to be his disciples.

Peter was frustrated after a long night of fishing and saw another net toss as a waste of time. But he showed faith in Jesus and obeyed. (v. 5) Then when the nets were ripping at the seams from the abundant fish trapped in them, they had a revelation of who he was. (vs. 9-10) Being the great leader that he was, Jesus seized on the moment and announced his vision: "From now on you'll be fishing for people!" (v 10). This was the moment where the idea of the big handprint was introduced to these men. They recognized what it was that Jesus was calling them to do and they couldn't resist.

> The disciples left everything (small footprint) so they could follow Jesus (big handprint).

The final event that occurs in this passage in Luke shows the essence of discipleship—and the heart behind small footprint, big handprint.

> "And as soon as they landed, they left everything and followed Jesus."
>
> — Luke 5:11

They left everything! Making a commitment to follow Jesus is the first step in the discipleship process. It's the beginning of the transformation of the mind. As we know, this transformation process isn't completed overnight, but it is the beginning of an adventure with God. These men left everything (small footprint) so they could follow Jesus (big handprint). Once we are truly following Jesus and walking out his commission to make disciples, we will make a lasting impact on the world.

One Command: Love

When we look at our world's major environmental crisis, the idea of a small footprint actually making a difference in the future seems somewhat daunting. And when we look at the way our society is so broken and fractured from shattered relationships to hollow pursuits dominating our lives, the idea of making authentic disciples who change the world seems idealistic at best. However, there is good news. God never calls us to do something that he doesn't equip us to do. In fact, he has given us the ability to fulfill both of these commissions with one simple command.

Love.

That's right—love. When our hearts become so connected to God's heart, we take on the things that are important to him. His creation is important to him; otherwise he wouldn't have saved it and given detailed instructions on how to do so. People are important to him; otherwise he wouldn't have sacrificed his son Jesus to have relationship with us. It was the answer to the question on all the Pharisees' minds during Jesus' time on earth.

> God never calls us to do something that he doesn't equip us to do. In fact, he has given us the ability to fulfill both of these commissions with one simple command.

"Teacher, which is the greatest commandment in the Law?" And he said to him, "You shall love the Lord your God with all your heart and with all your soul and with all your mind. This is the great and first commandment."
—Matthew 22:36-38

If we truly believe that God created this world and that he loves it, one of the ways we will express our love and appreciation of his love is caring for creation. That's our small footprint. We leave it behind in pristine condition for future generations to enjoy it as we have—or better yet, we restore it so that they can see more beauty and splendor than even we have even seen in this day and age. We're not trying to use up all the resources simply because we can; we're trying to preserve them because He loves this planet.

> If we truly believe that God created this world and that he loves it, one of the ways we will express our love and appreciation of his love is caring for creation.

If we truly know that God so loved us that He provided His son to save us for eternity, then we will obey his command to love people and tangibly demonstrate the Gospel by being the hands and feet of Jesus to a broken world. That's our handprint. We will walk out pure expressions of the Gospel and the world will not be able to resist it any longer.

Your Epitaph

If you want to figure out how committed you are to living a life of a small footprint and big handprint, ask yourself this question: What will they put on my tombstone?

You are writing your epitaph each day. The things you are doing, the events you are attending, the way you are living. The collective sum of our decisions is crafting what people will say about us after we die. Will people remark about your passion for God? Will people share stories of how your faith inspired them to pursue God with great passion? Will people mourn the loss of a man or woman who loved them when they were in their moment of greatest need for a true friend? Or will people even miss you at all? Will people remark about how successful you were and nothing more? Will your kids grind their teeth about what an absent father or a disinterested mother you were and gladly trade every dime of inheritance for quality time with you?

When we love God as Jesus challenged us to do, the inevitable result is that we experience a life of great adventure and faith with him, leaving behind a handprint that changed the world in which we lived and a footprint that went unnoticed.

Questions to Ponder

1. In what ways have you shown love toward creation?

2. How have you shown love toward others in the past week? What are you doing to create more opportunities to love others?

Small Footprint

Action point: Identify and eliminate one area of your lifestyle that you deem to be excessive, then ...

Big Footprint

Action Point: ... make a list of people you would like to begin showing love to but have never seized the opportunity—create some opportunities by inviting these people over for dinner or coffee and just listening to their story.

Looking Back

* There are two important commissions Jesus gave us: care for creation and make disciples.

* When we are truly following Jesus and walking out his commission to make disciples, we will make a lasting impact on the world.

* If you want to figure out how committed you are to living a life of a small footprint and big handprint, ask yourself this question: What will they put on my tombstone?

chapter five

Less External Complexity

How our stuff creates barriers
to leaving a big handprint

"It's difficult for people to get rid of junk. They get attached to things and let them define who they are. If there's one thing I've learned in this business, it's that you are what you can't let go of."
– Brian Scudamore, CEO of 1-800-GOT-JUNK

But as I looked at everything I had worked so hard to accomplish, it was all so meaningless. It was like chasing the wind. There was nothing really worthwhile anywhere.
– Ecclesiastes 2:11

enry David Thoreau once wrote, "Simplicity, simplicity, simplicity! I say, let your affairs be as two or three, and not a hundred or a thousand; instead of a million count half a dozen, and keep your accounts on your thumb nail ... simplicity, simplicity. Instead of three meals a day, if it be necessary eat but one; instead of a hundred dishes, five; and reduce other things in proportion."

This might be one of the most famous quotes Thoreau wrote while spending a year of solitude and contemplation in a small cabin in the woods on Walden's Pond. Although not a Christian writer, Thoreau tapped into a biblical truth; what really counts in life can't be found or claimed with too great of distraction. Over and over again the Gospel writers noted how many times Jesus went to the mountain or to places of solitude to spend time with the Father in order to get direction and clarity. Complexity has a way of distracting us from simple truth and peace.

The world constantly communicates that we need to buy more material possessions to make our lives easier. Ironically, they are some of the very things that have a tendency to clutter our lives. Rarely do we return from a trip to the store without bringing home something we couldn't possibly live without. Those "things" generally end up on shelves untouched or unused until it is time to make room for more unneeded possessions, at which time they are removed and discarded. In this day it takes great discipline not to be duped by advertising and clever displays. It is much like the discipline of passing by a plate of chocolate during the holiday season knowing that the momentary pleasure of taste will be outlasted by the addition of unwanted calories.

The complex life often leads us unexpectedly to financial stress. We want things, so we find ourselves conveniently buying "on time," promising to pay it back later. In today's world of financial bondage, you can find a payday loan store on every corner or easy money at high interest just fingertips away. So begins the long spiraling journey into overwhelming complexities that can ruin a couple's marriage, destroy someone's credit, and steal anyone's joy. Who really wants to live this way?

Telling Commodities

If you want to figure out what's actually important to you instead of what you say is important, just look at how you spend two things: your time and your money. The results of your personal survey may be chilling. These two elements either create the external complexity that muddles our lives or they are merely an indicator of the enduring freedom we have to respond to God's call on our lives.

So often when the topic of simplifying our lives is broached, it begins and ends with finances. And while there is more to external complexity than money, it remains a good starting place. Jesus said it simply: "No one can serve two masters ... You can not serve both God and money" (Luke 16:13). Too many people serve money because they mistakenly believe that life is all about how much you accumulate. But life is temporary and short—and we're not going to take anything with us. So why spend the bulk of your life trying to amass stuff you'll leave behind anyway? Why not open your hand and let go of material things, allowing yourself to leave the biggest handprint possible?

> If most people's lives aren't about pursuing money, then they're most certainly about pursuing happiness.

King Solomon, the wisest man in the Bible, gained some of his wisdom through trial and error. Although we like to think of him as this all-knowing sage, the truth is that while he may have possessed some God-given wisdom, his experiences along with his ability to learn from them marked the great life lessons he passed along. Solomon writes, "Those who love money will never have enough. How absurd to think that wealth brings true happiness!" (Ecclesiastes 5:10).

If most people's lives aren't about pursuing money, then they're most certainly about pursuing happiness. We invest our time in things that we think will bring us joy or happiness, when in the end it's merely a way to pass the precious time we've been given here in this lifetime. I've seen countless friends abandon all responsibilities and commitments because they think doing something else will make them happy. In the end, the emptiness remains—along with a more complex mess created by their inability to be content with what they have, both tangible and intangible.

We don't have to travel down a path with this type of maddening unattainable destination. Just read what one of the wealthiest kings in the history of Israel had to say about such vain pursuits:

> I also tried to find meaning by building huge homes for myself and by planting beautiful vineyards. I made gardens and parks, filling them with all kinds of fruit trees. I built reservoirs to collect the water to irrigate my many flourishing groves. I bought slaves, both men and women, and others were born into my household. I also owned great herds and flocks, more than any of the kings who lived in Jerusalem before me. I collected great sums of silver and gold, the treasure of many kings and provinces. I hired wonderful singers, both men and women, and had many beautiful concubines. I had everything a man could desire! So I became greater than any of the kings who ruled in Jerusalem before me. And with it all, I remained clear-eyed so that I could evaluate all these things. Anything I wanted, I took. I did not restrain myself from any joy. I even found great pleasure in hard work, an additional reward for all my labors. But as I looked at everything I had worked so hard to accomplish, it was all so meaningless. It was like chasing the wind. There was nothing really worthwhile anywhere.
>
> – Ecclesiastes 2:4-11

The same things that complicated Solomon's life thousands of years ago can complicate ours today. Putting personal comfort and security ahead of God will undoubtedly complicate our lives. Becoming entangled in work and busy schedules will complicate our lives. Allowing money and power to override simple obedience will complicate our lives. Becoming entangled in unhealthy relationships will complicate our lives.

One of the greatest tragedies in humanity is for a person to come to the end of his or her life and realize that it was misspent. Unused gifts will lead to an empty life. Of course, God gives us the free will to use the talents He gives us as we choose. But not using something for its purpose will only create frustration and aggravation. Is your life being well spent? Are your talents being used according to the purposes God designed them for? Are you enjoying the freedom that comes from existing in a place where you are in harmony with God and His calling for your life through simple living? If not, here are a few suggestions to help you get rid of the external complexities plaguing you and to help you begin walking in the freedom that allows you to make a big handprint on the world around you through practically demonstrating God's love and grace.

> One of the greatest tragedies in humanity is for a person to come to the end of his or her life and realize that it was misspent.

Three Good Ideas

Reevaluate. By now, you have probably already begun the process of re-evaluating your life as you've pondered the first few chapters of this book. If you haven't gone deep, and this process has been merely a cursory thought for you, let's get more intentional and go deeper.

Here are some questions that should help you take inventory of where you are when it comes to external complexity:

1. Has my life become too complex and complicated?

2. How am I investing my life?

3. Am I spending this great gift of life the very best way possible?

4. Do I constantly talk about wanting more time when it comes to tasks that are meaningful as opposed to ones that aren't?

5. Do I find it difficult to do things that I would love—and make a difference in others' lives—rather than those that I feel obligated to do?

When reflecting on the state of your life, there are three points of evaluation to consider: time, energy (emotional and physical), and money. Those areas create a snapshot of what your life looks like—and what needs to change if you want to simplify your life and love extravagantly. Those three elements seem to define extravagance when you heap them upon others; therefore, taking careful inventory of them is paramount when re-evaluating your current life.

In the midst of my desire to really gain a good grasp on what it means to live a simplified life, my wife and I traveled to Indiana near the heart of the state's Amish community. As my wife and I drove into town, there was an Amish church with a sign that read: "JOY – Jesus first, Others second, You last." That little phrase encapsulated why the Amish people live the way they do. In some of my conversations with the people in this community, I discovered that their choice to continue using horses and buggies as a mode of transportation was because motorized vehicles took them too far away from family. Television disrupted their family time. There was purpose behind every decision to maintain the simplified life they lead in a complicated world.

Now, I'm not advocating that living an Amish lifestyle is the goal for the Christian life. However, reflecting upon their deeply held convictions and beliefs should challenge Christians to ponder this question: Are you set apart? The Amish people are set apart because of the way they choose to live. But are you really that committed to Christ that your life reflects uniqueness in Christ or do you just blend in with everyone else? As you take inventory of your time, energy and money, that question should be overlaid at each point of re-evaluation: Does the way you spend your time reflect your passion and commitment to Christ? Does the way you expend your energy reflect your passion and commitment to Christ? Does the way you spend your money reflect your passion and commitment to Christ?

Refocus and reprioritize. One afternoon, I was out in our yard, pruning rose bushes with Nancy. I was operating the clippers and she was directing. At one point, she wanted me to cut back what I thought was an excessive amount of a branch. I could see all this growth above the point she wanted me to cut back. As I protested, she told me it was necessary and asked me to trust her. So, I did—and a few weeks later, I couldn't believe the results! The rose bushes were almost dead the year before, but now they were gorgeous in full bloom.

> As you seek to refocus your life, ask yourself this question: What needs pruning in my life?

As you seek to refocus your life, ask yourself this question: What needs pruning in my life? Certainly as you begin to take stock of you life, things will jump out at you as needing to be eliminated or cut back. Consider Jesus' words in the book of John:

I am the true vine, and my Father is the gardener. He cuts off every branch that doesn't produce fruit, and he prunes the branches that do not bear fruit so they will produce even more.

You have already been pruned for greater fruitfulness by the message I have given you. Remain in me, and I will remain in you. For a branch cannot produce fruit if it is severed from the vine, and you cannot be fruitful apart from me.

– John 15:1-4

In order to refocus, ask yourself this question: What in my life needs to go? There are always areas you can weed out that you may upon first glance believe that they are necessary—but they aren't. The only way to get more out of life is to choose less—less stuff, less unnecessary activities, less of wanting more, less of self. Life on earth is temporary and short. We came into the world with nothing and we'll leave with nothing; so, why do we spend the bulk of our lives trying to accumulate material things?

Reorganize. At this point, reorganization occurs when you begin implementing the decisions you've made from what's most important to what's least important. I wish I had gone through this process in my 20s instead of waiting until I was in my 50s to do this. If you're in the same stage of life as me, you're probably thinking, *What about retirement? Pension? How will I spend the rest of my life?* But it's precisely at this point of evaluation that you have to decide what's more important to you. And more importantly—what's most important to God? How do you want to spend the life he has given you? I want to spend the rest of my life on this earth concentrating on my family and marriage and the community that God has given me. Those are the things that last—not the junk we acquire or monuments we try to build for ourselves. If you're from a younger generation, understand that the longer you go weaving a web of complexity in your life, the more difficult it will be to untangle it down the road.

Three Key Components of Reorganization

As mentioned earlier in this chapter, time, energy (emotional and physical), and money are three key components in the reorganization of your life. Let's take a look at how we can reorganize those areas.

Time. Psalm 90:12 says, "Teach us to make the most of our time, so that we may grow in wisdom." Of all the commodities we have, time is the one that is always dwindling away no matter what we do. There are no "roll-over minutes" with God, which is why we must treat our time so special. In the average day, week or month, I'm sure you will discover time wasters that amount to nothing, not even a relaxing moment. So, why allow that into your life?

Begin this exercise of reorganization by asking tough, but helpful questions:

* What can I eliminate from my schedule?
* What is in my schedule due to my guilt or my inability to say "no"?
* What good is coming out of the way I spend my extra time? (i.e. Am I building others up? Being built up myself? Encouraging others? Being encouraged? Getting time to clear my head and think or hear from God?)

> We need to reorganize our lives so we may put more into it, leaving a big handprint that puts a permanent impression of God's love on the lives of those around us.

People have written plenty of books on this topic, giving us ways to organize our lives in an effort to get more out of it. However, I'm advocating that we reorganize our lives so we may *put more into it*, leaving a big handprint that puts a permanent impression of God's love on the lives of those around us. We do this by beginning to learn to say "no" to good things in order for us to participate in the truly great things our hearts are stirred to do by the Creator.

Energy. Unlike time, energy is actually a

renewable resource we have, but it isn't inexhaustible. However, many people enter into a place of burnout because they are investing their energy in the wrong things, things that suck them dry as opposed to reinvigorating them with life. It's a sinking feeling to know you've been wasting your energy on something that's going nowhere.

Have you ever gone on a cleaning binge where you proceeded to throw out or give away items you once held as your valuable possessions but now deemed junk? If you've never done this, you're missing out. If you have, you understand how incredibly freeing this process is. You know you'll never have to lug that extra "thing" around ever again. It's gone. In many ways, spring cleaning is a great picture for what God wants us to do when it come to reorganizing our lives. We need to purge our activities so that we have energy to do the things that we love most and count exponentially longer. (Hobbies and "down time" are important and God definitely wants us to enjoy the life He has given us—it just shouldn't consume us.) We also need to take inventory of those relationships that are sucking us dry. Sometimes we need to spend extra time with a friend or acquaintance, but we must also be diligent to set boundaries so that those relationships don't consume all our energy.

> Simplicity is the antidote to feeling overwhelmed.

Simplicity is the antidote to feeling overwhelmed. When it comes to our energy, we sometimes move from one feeling of being overwhelmed to the next, whether it be from our workload or our relationships. God wants us to render our lives down so we're not living in this constant state of chaos and stress. It's hard to demonstrate God's love in practical ways if you don't have the time or energy to sense His love in your own life.

Money. This is often the hardest cycle for people to get out of because they have to change their lifestyle. You have to take your eyes off the get-rich-quick schemes and set them on a get-out-of-debt-quick plan. You're not going to get anywhere if you don't make a plan—and paring down your budget in order to do this can be painful. But it can be done.

After we taught through this topic at our church, we have heard story after story of couples who got out of major debt through simplifying their lifestyle. We equipped people with ways to do this through training and teaching, encouraging them to discover a new way to live. Enrolling in one of Dave Ramsey's Financial Peace University at a local church is a great place to start.[1] The stories of people in our church who went through this program and the changes they made always make a profound impact on others when they share how they did it and, more importantly, why they did it.

> One truth I have discovered is that possessions have a way of taking ownership of our lives.

If you're in debt, make a plan to become debt-free so that money no longer occupies your mind and distracts you from the things that really matter. Look at how you spend your money on a monthly basis and ask yourself what things are really necessary and what things are not. One truth I have discovered is that possessions have a way of taking ownership of our lives.

Once, Nancy and I owned an old boat that my son Brook and I restored. We found great joy working together to make it seaworthy. We dreamed of the day we would put it on some lake and speed across to distant places. The project took us two years to complete, but finally after a number of failed attempts the boat was ready. We used it a good deal for the next year or two, but eventually it just sat in its relegated spot, as other recreational activities took our attention and interest away. The boat had become just another "toy" that made us feel guilty when we weren't using it. At times, I found myself working on it, keeping it maintained so it was ready for use. But for the most part, it just sat there in the way. The joy was found in the creativity of the project, the richness of working together with our hands. It was the dream of what it could be rather than the possession of something that eventually owned us. I have discovered that many "toys" are like that.

The author of Proverbs begged two favors of God before he died. First, he asked, "… help me never to tell a lie. Second, give me neither poverty nor riches! Give me just enough to satisfy my needs. For if I grow rich, I may deny you and say, 'Who is the Lord?' And if I am too poor, I may steal and thus insult God's holy name" (Proverbs 30:7).

Simplifying your physical life in the areas of finances and possessions is anything but simple—it will take planning and work. But it will help you to discover a new freedom and a peace that you probably haven't experienced in a long time.

External complexities have plenty of trappings if we're not careful. But if we're diligent about taking time once a year to re-evaluate, refocus and reprioritize, and reorganize our lives, we'll find that it's easier to shirk those trappings than we might think.

Questions to Ponder

1. What are some things—time commitments, possessions, etc.—that you could do without?

2. What does the way you spend your money personally reflect your priorities? Are those the same things you want reflected as your top priority?

Small Footprint

Action point: Write down a list of your weekly and monthly time commitments and eliminate one from your schedule and...

Big Footprint

Action Point: ... find one organization or opportunity you are passionate about and donate half (or all) of your new freed up time there.

Looking Back

* Begin getting rid of external complexities by re-evaluating, refocusing and reprioritizing, and reorganizing.

* Three key components to assess in reorganizing your life are time, money and energy.

* God wants us to render our lives down so we're not living in this constant state of chaos and stress. Simplicity is the antidote to feeling overwhelmed.

chapter six

Less Internal Complexity

Making more room for God to work

*"Thou hast created us for Thyself, and our heart is not
quiet until it rests in Thee."*
— St. Augustine

*Submit yourselves, then, to God. Resist the devil, and
he will flee from you. Come near to God and he will
come near to you. Wash your hands, you sinners, and
purify your hearts, you double-minded. Grieve, mourn
and wail. Change your laughter to mourning and
your joy to gloom.*
— James 4:7-9

've always been a bit meticulous about being on time to everything. Perhaps it was the people I worked under when I was younger, but being late was never an option—in fact, it's best to be early, if anything. This ideal created the reason for my angst one morning as I drove my 1965 VW bug to work across the southern California desert to Lancaster where I served on a church staff. When being on time is deeply important to you, you know little things like exactly how long it would take to get from your driveway to work. And on this morning, my margin for arriving on time was razor thin.

As I drove, my mind drifted to some of the looming decisions we had to make as a church staff. Situations were complicated and a clear answer seemed to avoid everyone. Nevertheless, I thought about them and wondered if we would come up with the right solution. In the midst of my thought process, I felt the Lord prompting me to stop my wagon and climb atop a 500-foot butte rising up out of the middle of the desert. Suddenly, I had a problem with what God was saying. I thought, *I can't be late. Surely, God knows what time it is!* I began arguing with God, but it ended quickly when I felt Him impressing so strongly upon me that I needed to obey and realized this wasn't going away.

Reluctantly, I drove to the base of the butte and climbed to the top of it, not quite sure why God was asking me to do this. In those days, to operate in that kind of obedience was radical for me. As I reached the top, I looked around in all four directions and then sat on a rock. The sun was just piercing the early morning horizon when I heard the Lord clearly speak to me regarding the situation we were facing at the church. The Lord gave me a prayer for my pastor—it was simple; just two sentences. But I had this complete peace when I finished. In this place of complete solitude, God spoke to me something simple and profound that would change everything in the hours to come.

When I finally arrived at the church, I was the first one there as the entire staff suffered from acute tardiness that morning. In our meeting, I shared the prayer that the Lord had given me for our pastor—and it was indeed the perfect prayer for that moment. The confusion that shrouded our pastor broke over him and we quickly were able to navigate through the troubled waters with wisdom and success.

That morning I learned a great lesson: If God is calling you out of your busy frantic schedule, obey Him and step out in obedience. To make a difference in any situation, you must make yourself available to hear God's voice. That lesson has always stuck with me and I've been determined to practice it ever since. Things can look simple and well-organized on the outside, but if our insides are all twisted up with complexity, we still face the daunting task of being able to love others extravagantly. Internal complexity usually means we need healing and maturity. It's hard to see who we need to share God's love with when our eyes are on ourselves.

> It's hard to see who we need to share God's love with when our eyes are on ourselves. ... We've got to get beyond ourselves and let Jesus have his way with our lives.

Whatever Christians have been doing hasn't been working effectively. If it did work, the divorce rate among Christians wouldn't be just as high as the rest of the world's divorce rate. If it did work, churches would be organizations whose focus would be on changing the world through changed lives, not organizations of "cool" where one-upmanship centers around the "hottest" worship leader or the latest techno gadget to draw nothing more than large crowds. If it did work, we would have our noses buried in "let's go change the world" books in between changing it, not seeking out the best-selling self-help book. We've got to get beyond ourselves and let Jesus have his way with our lives. Quit bemoaning your situation and take advantage of the provision made available to us through the cross. Start living like a new creation for creation's sake. It's easy to get stuck in our navel-gazing-obsessed society. However, when we render down all these internal complexities, we can get on with God's call to love other people. We must become less so that our lives will be free to give more. This is a key ingredient and motive for a smaller footprint.

From Chaos to Harmony

A life leaving a small footprint is one that understands the beauty—and necessity—of simplicity. And there is nothing that damages a simplified life more than being a complex person. Internal conflict is the great thief of tranquility. When our life is out of sorts with God or others, everything else is out of sync—the natural rhythm is gone. If we are dealing with issues of guilt, shame, anger or rage, we can become paralyzed, losing the freedom to pursue the dream of inner peace and a simplified life in its purest sense. Unresolved issues cause us to lose our vision for the pursuit of a life with the freedom to initiate change; simplicity requires a commitment to all kinds of change.

> Internal conflict is the great thief of tranquility.

The simplified life—one that is marked by a small footprint—is a life that moves into harmony not just with the natural environment, but also with personal relationships and most importantly with God. Through our relationship with God, He gives us freedom, healing and a new beginning, all of which are prerequisites to a life of peace. Jesus' stated mission was "to set the captive free"[1] and we all have been captive one way or another due to sin. This may be because of our own sin or because we have been sinned against. These bad choices and actions have stifled our lives and paralyzed our vision, putting us into a perpetual state of status quo. Our only hope for change is found in the provision of Christ. Through this incredible gift of grace, we can experience the forgiveness, healing and freedom to restore our wounds, our marriages and important relationships.

One reality I've discovered is that if Nancy and I don't have harmony in our marriage, we lose our ability to share vision. Sin and unresolved issues can cause us to focus inward, and we lose sight of our preferred future together. The times we seem to move ahead the most expediently are the times when we are both experiencing internal freedom. It is because of this that Christ must be central in our relationship together. When we are free, we can dream together of our future and plan how to get there. I love those times because they are challenging, exciting and empowering. When we are evenly yoked together in vision there is no call from the Lord so great that we can't answer. A life of simplicity requires vision—vision requires freedom, freedom that is only available in Christ.

Consider the words of James, who found himself ministering to people caught in the complexities of relationships and life:

What is causing the quarrels and fights among you? Isn't it the whole army of evil desires at war within you? You want what you don't have, so you scheme and kill to get it. You are jealous for what others have, and you can't possess it, so you fight and quarrel to take it away from them. And yet the reason you don't have what you want is that you don't ask God for it. And even when you do ask, you don't get it because your whole motive is wrong you want only what will give you pleasure. You adulterers! Don't you realize that friendship with this world makes you an enemy of God? I say it again, that if your aim is to enjoy this world, you can't be a friend of God. What do you think the Scriptures mean when they say that the Holy Spirit, whom God has placed within us, jealously longs for us to be faithful? He gives us more and more strength to stand against such evil desires. As the Scriptures say, "God sets himself against the proud, but he shows favor to the humble." So humble yourselves before God. Resist the Devil, and he will flee from you. Draw close to God, and God will draw close to you. Wash your hands, you sinners; purify your hearts, you hypocrites. Let there be tears for the wrong things you have done. Let there be sorrow and deep grief. Let there be sadness instead of laughter, and gloom instead of joy. When you bow down before the Lord and admit your dependence on him, he will lift you up and give you honor.

— James 4:1-10 (NIV)

In this text, James makes an impassioned plea to his readers to leave behind the chaotic life the world offers for one of peace where utter dependence upon God brings us to a place of simplicity and freedom. James explains the process of moving from one place (chaos) to another (dependence upon God). Let's unpack this wise passage and follow its path.

1. Don't confuse simple with easy. The human condition is prone to suffering and adversity—there's no way around it. However, a life of internal simplicity is not marked as being easy. There are trials; there are tribulations; there are moments of turmoil. Instead of dismissing these ideas, James challenges us to consider the source of these complexities: What is causing the quarrels? What evil lurks within?

Many people make the mistake of trying to create an easier life, believing that is the path to simplicity. Aside from their bickering, these people are coveting their neighbors' possessions. And when they do decide to ask God for something, their motives are wrong—they're out for pleasure and merely to enjoy the world. Life can be simple yet difficult at times.

> Many people make the mistake of trying to create an easier life, believing that is the path to simplicity.

2. Admit that you are in a "battle within." James asks the readers to acknowledge that "the whole army of evil desires is at war within you" (v. 1). The inner war we face is the battle for our soul.

Though we may give our lives to Jesus, our hearts are continually bombarded and wooed by the enemy—anything to distract us from fulfilling the potential God has for us. Once we recognize this war raging within us, we must evaluate the motives of our heart. (see vs. 3) Why are we doing what we're doing? What is the purpose behind our decisions? Then we must ask what is driving our thoughts, attitudes, anger and resentment. Understanding the battle we face internally is incredibly crucial to winning it.

3. Make a choice for freedom—and ask God for help. For some of us, the movie *Groundhog Day* isn't such a laughing matter when we think about it in terms of our lives. We sometimes feel trapped in this perpetual cycle of sin. We are tempted and know we should resist. We give in and do it anyway. We feel shame and guilt so we don't tell anyone about it. Then we do it again. James implores his readers to break free of this cycle by asking God for help. "Draw close to God, and God will draw close to you" (v. 8). Throughout the New Testament, there are verses describing the effects of sinful behavior and the reality of cyclical sin.[2]

4. Recognize how you have been held captive by the world's way of dealing with pain. There are many ways people do this, some of which we easily recognize as wrong, while others are acceptable. For example, we denounce self-medicating with alcohol as wrong. But overeating or going on rampant shopping sprees are seen as acceptable ways of dealing with the blues. In Romans 12, Paul writes that we shouldn't be conformed to this world, but transformed. Will we self-medicate the way the world does? Or will we get on our knees and seek peace and strength from God when facing stressful or difficult times? Behaving like the rest of the world, when faced with pain, only creates more complexity in our lives. At some point we will still have to deal with our pain. The simple way is to cope by seeking God's help. Some of my more spiritual prayers go like this: "God, help me! I can't do this on my own!" It may not be the most eloquent of prayers, but who cares? When I feel stuck and held captive in the world's way of dealing with pain, I cry out to God to help me. And he does.

5. Repentance begins with humility and brokenness. The final step in moving to dependence upon God starts with a contrite heart. Instead of thinking we can do it all by ourselves, we realize that God isn't just a good idea, and we need Him. Consider Paul's words when writing to the church in Corinth over their plight:

> Yet now I am happy, not because you were made sorry, but because your sorrow led you to repentance. For you became sorrowful as God intended and so were not harmed in any way by us. Godly sorrow brings repentance that leads to salvation and leaves no regret, but worldly sorrow brings death.
> – 2 Corinthians 7:9-10 (NIV)

A broken heart is broken soil, a place where life can spring forth when tended properly. We can't just laugh off the tough times and pain in our lives, whether the wounds are self-inflicted or induced by others. Once we do that, we properly nurture this soil through confession—a cleaning out of the dark closets in our soul. This is a wise and necessary step: "He who conceals his sins does not prosper, but whoever confesses and renounces them finds mercy" (Proverbs 28:13). This leads us to a state of true repentance, which is when we feel the full impact of turning away from our sins and turning to God's unconditional love, mercy and forgiveness.

David was a man who experienced true repentance. Reflect for a moment about the depths to which he sank in his life (adulterer and murderer) before reading how he felt as he basked in God's incredible love and forgiveness:

Come and listen, all you who fear God; let me tell you what he has done for me. I cried out to him with my mouth; his praise was on my tongue. If I had cherished sin in my heart, the Lord would not have listened; but God has surely listened and heard my voice in prayer. Praise be to God, who has not rejected my prayer or withheld his love from me!

– Psalm 66:16-20

Jesus came to free us from our confusion and to give us a true sense of identity. He fills the believer with his Spirit to give us inner peace as a person so that we are no longer motivated to frantically try to discover ourselves. With his Spirit comes the fruit of a righteous character, integrity and behavior. Paul wrote, "When the Holy Spirit controls our lives, he will produce this kind of fruit in us: love, joy, peace, patience, kindness, goodness, faithfulness, gentleness, and self-control" (Galatians 5:22).

The fruits of the Spirit will provide the kind of attributes that will bring harmony to our lives, allowing us to be consistent and stable no matter what the circumstance or station of life. Only then will we be people for all seasons—unchanged by the pressures of a society continually trying to get us to conform to the world's way of thinking about who we should be and how we should act. Instead we will daily yield ourselves to the process of being transformed into Christ's image. This is "Christ-likeness" and it is the only way to find internal tranquility and being at peace with who we are. It is a prerequisite for the life of simplicity. We all want to walk in freedom—and it's through freedom that we are able to make a bigger impact on others through our lives.

In this journey toward freedom, we must remember that remaining in a place of freedom doesn't just happen. The enemy is forever trying to thwart God's best plan for your life through temptation and the lure of "something better." Once we taste freedom, we must understand that the only way to remain in that place is through the disciplined practice of spending time deepening our relationship with God.

Why does practicing spiritual disciplines matter?

As we attempt to unravel the internal complexity in our lives, we must move forward by determining to hear God's voice speaking into our lives. Far too many people want a cookie-cutter approach to defining their relationship with God. But formulas don't work in relationship—and since God made us all different and unique, it would be disingenuous to present a blanket plan to nurture your relationship with Him. We need to hear God's voice for our lives because what's simple for me may be difficult for you. Practicing spiritual disciplines allows us to get before God and hear what He has to say about unraveling the complexity in our lives as opposed to some five-point formula that almost dismisses God entirely from the process.

Placing God at the center of our spiritual discipline is the only way we will ever succeed in developing the habit in our lives that will lead to a greater sense of peace and understanding about what He has in store for us. That may sound simple—and that's exactly the point. We have a tendency to make things much more complicated than they need to be if we're not careful.

So, for the sake of simplicity and the fact that there are already some great books out there about spiritual disciplines (*The Celebration of Discipline* by Richard Foster being one of the best), let's answer the two most pressing questions.

Question #1: **How should I "be"?**

The enemy will do anything he can to prevent us from coming to a place of stillness so God might speak to us and tell us what we need to know. God is not trying to hide from us. He wants to impart wisdom and direction to us—if we'll only listen. In order to learn how we should "be", we must come to God with these types of questions:

- "Lord, how should I be in this situation?"
- "And how should I respond out of that state of being with you?"

People often tell me, "I have tried this silence thing or solitude thing and it just doesn't work for me. It's just so abnormal for me to be silent. I just can't do it." In our culture, it is difficult to achieve silence. However, we must be diligent to do so. We can find many answers about how to be by reading God's Word. But there are times when the answers aren't so black and white. We need to hear him speak to us both through his Word and through prayer where we take the time to listen for his voice.

We have to figure out a way to get some time with God, regardless of our situation or place in life. Perhaps you're in college and getting up early seems like nothing more than a noble idea; then try carving out some time around lunch to get quiet before God and ask him these questions. Or maybe you're a mother with toddlers and the thought of peace with God seems as doable as buying out Bill Gates. Create some space in your day wherever possible—maybe during naptime for your kids—and seek God. Your situation may not be ideal or what you wished it would be, but those moments alone with God will prove invaluable.

At my stage in life, I'm able to spend an hour each morning sitting in front of my window and simply listening to God. I don't even strive in prayer. I just sit and wait and listen. It's what I do before I do anything (except maybe brew a pot of coffee). I take all of the issues pressing on my heart to him and just listen. I let him do the talking—and it has worked wonders for me in my relationship with Him and in refining my leadership skills.

Question #2: **How do I get there?**

In order to be connected to God and get where we want to go in our spiritual journey, we have to make time for him. This can be difficult at times. A recent *Time* magazine article, Dr. Donald Roberts, a communications professor from Stanford, explained the difficulty facing our culture when it comes to being still: "It seems to me that there's almost a discomfort with not being stimulated—a kind of 'I can't stand the silence.'"[3] Once we know what God is calling us to do, we can go in confidence that he is with us.

Relinquishing control of our lives to God is the key, which only comes when we obediently follow God's direction for our lives. Being controlled by the Holy Spirit sounds rather strange. But this isn't the type of control where someone makes you do things you don't want to do—this is the kind of guidance and direction we seek all our lives. When we're in touch with the Holy Spirit and he is leading us each day to make the right choices in the middle of conflict, we're learning to be exactly the way God wants us to be. We begin to walk out authentic Christianity where we're not thrashing others around us and having outbursts of anger or fits of rage. We're at peace and calmly handling the situation. We arrive at a place of internal peace and contentment because the Holy Spirit is leading and guiding us. This is our target and with his help we will reach it.

> Relinquishing control of our lives to God is the key, which only comes when we obediently follow God's direction for our lives.

However, we must be leery of falling into the trap that rescues simplicity movements only to later end them altogether. Most movements of simplicity become inwardly focused in order to remain that way. Most groups of people committed to the simplified life have had to make rules and regulations—and they had to be cookie-cutter. In most cases, simplicity morphed into legalism. Though a fictional story, M. Night Shyamalan's movie *The Village* depicts clearly how this can occur within a society. When you have rules and laws, Paul tells us in Romans that we can't keep them and we eventually fall into shame and condemnation. So many groups have tried to achieve simplicity, but have failed in terms of trying to fulfill one of the major directives of Jesus: Love your neighbor. We struggle to blend the ideal of simplicity with that of having a heart for the world around us and actually doing something about it.

The Simplicity of Spiritual Disciplines

Although there is no absolute list of spiritual disciplines, here are some of the more obvious ones for the benefit of understanding why they are an essential part of the simplified life, especially as it pertains to lessening our internal complexities.

Solitude. Solitude helps us get in touch with ourselves. It is during times of solitude that we can hear God and receive vision and direction for our lives as well as reminders of our priorities. I generally begin each day with at least an hour of complete silence. I have found that it empowers me for a much more efficient and effective day. Silence requires as little distraction as possible and works best when there is a complete absence of noise (not even worship music) or visual distraction (Bible reading is yet another discipline). Solitude should be a daily event, but on occasion can be given to a longer special time in a more remote place. Most people confess that their schedule doesn't allow the luxury of solitude, but that very confession is the motivation for writing about this topic concerning the simplified life. Even if it's five minutes in the bathroom, find a way to make it happen.

Prayer. This is not the kind of prayer that goes with meals or formalities; rather, it is the prayer connected to solitude. Sometimes we not only listen to God for our lives, but we have to have the faith to believe that he in turn hears us. The apostle Paul said, "Do not be anxious about anything, but in everything, by prayer and petition, with thanksgiving, present your requests to God. And the peace of God, which transcends all understanding, will guard your hearts and your minds in Christ Jesus" (Philippians 4:6). This is not only a perfect model for prayer, petition, and thanksgiving, but Paul also points out that prayer is the avenue to peace and the absence of anxiety. These are essential qualities for a life of simplicity.

Reading the Bible. The discipline of consistent Bible reading reveals God's heart for us and thus leads us to healing and freedom. The Word of God is living and active and can penetrate our innermost being like a sharp double-edged sword. (Hebrews 4:12) It is always relevant no matter where we are in life; it will speak to our heart's condition and God's unfailing love for us.

Fellowship, community and service. These are three more spiritual disciplines necessary for a more basic and simplified lifestyle. In the early days of our nation the Church not only provided access to a spiritual life, but it provided the major part of social and recreational life. People helped each other cut wood to keep their homes warm against the winter; men and children worked side by side harvesting crops; and women canned food together to store up provisions. It was a time when life was more basic, but then that's what this topic of the simplified life is all about. Not that we need to practice these past skills necessarily, but young mothers still need the wisdom of the older women, and young men still need the accountability of older men.

There is something rich about the operation of all these spiritual disciplines that is basic to our human needs and is part of the provision of Christ through his Church. Each of these disciplines adds to the fullness of a life lived in Christ and must be things we build into our everyday lives.

Questions to Ponder

1. What issues in your life have created internal complexities? Why?

2. How can you lessen your internal complexities through some of the ideas mentioned in this chapter?

Small Footprint

Action point: From your answers to the questions above, pick one of the ideas and follow through in order to create more internal simplicity so you might...

Big Footprint

Action Point: ...be able to pour into others. Ask God to show you a person in your life who needs some encouragement and take them to lunch or coffee and tell this person all the things about them that you appreciate.

Looking Back

* It's hard to give others love from the well of life when we're bone dry on the inside.

* Don't confuse simple with easy. Life can be simple yet still difficult at the same time.

* We must get before God each day and ask "How should I be?" and "How do I get there?". That's how we will begin to reduce our internal complexity.

chapter seven

More Preparedness

Being ready creates opportunity
for bigger handprints

"If you aim at nothing, you will hit it every time."
– Zig Ziglar

Wise planning will watch over you. Understanding
will keep you safe.
– Proverbs 2:11

Thanks to Rick Warren, these days it's difficult to find people who don't believe God has purpose for their lives. His best-selling book *The Purpose-Driven Life* opened people's eyes to this simple truth. In our effort to leave a small footprint but a big handprint on the world, what do we do with the knowledge that God has plans for our lives? If God has purpose for our lives, he also has ways and means to execute his plans. However, that doesn't mean we stand by and do nothing. When we fail to develop a plan for our lives, life has a tendency to control us, putting us at the mercy of a system, rather than giving us the opportunity to make decisions that will help us accomplish the plan we believe God has for us. A big handprint requires a plan—and it won't happen by itself or with wishful thinking. You must act on it.

The week after Hurricane Katrina hit New Orleans in 2005, I managed to find a way to get into the city with another pastor friend of mine from Seattle and our sons. We borrowed an army supply truck from a church in Baton Rouge and drove past military checkpoints with goods to help people. I went there to develop a plan, determining what the greatest needs were for disaster relief teams headed to New Orleans from our church in Boise. In the midst of chaos, I realized again how the idea of vision and strategic planning is crucial for those desiring to make a big handprint on the world. I found that the organizations, groups and people who were prepared and ready ahead of time for such a disaster were the ones making a difference in their respective communities. I also observed that people who put all of their faith in a system experienced disappointment. Many people in the Gulf Coast region of Louisiana and Mississippi put all their faith in insurance companies and the government and believed they would subsidize all their losses. Unfortunately, stories of tragic loss and inability to receive financial help became all too common in the aftermath of the storm's wake. Witnessing this firsthand only underscored my reason for being there—and the reason why strategic planning and vision are so important to making a big handprint.

We live in a world that is increasingly unstable, which is why we must be attentive to God's voice in our lives. When we move from understanding we have a purpose to living out our purpose; asking God for help and direction in developing a plan is actually vital if we intend to change the world. The great challenge of living a simplified life is remembering to slow down long enough to ask God those questions and begin to develop a plan to get there. Thinking ahead is paramount. If we don't think ahead, the complexities of life will overwhelm us and begin to control our finances, resources and daily schedules.

To enter into a simplified life that will leave a big handprint, we have to ask ourselves this question: "What do I want to accomplish in this window of opportunity called life on earth?"

Culture of Preparedness

There are two ways Christian leaders can respond to crisis or the potential of it. They can fear it and try to avoid it at all cost, or they can use it for the advantage and advancement of God's Kingdom. Even when it comes to the Christian response to eschatological views of the last days or end times prophecy, people often respond differently. Some build a theology to be raptured before they personally have to face troubled times, and some see it as an opportune time to be right on the frontlines of evangelism, knowing that in the midst of tough times people are most receptive to the hope of eternity. There will always be different responses to conflict and human suffering, but the great leaders I have researched throughout the years seemed to see the potential in every situation both good and bad. Difficulty most often sets a stage of opportunity for those who desire to make

> Difficulty most often sets a stage of opportunity for those who desire to make the biggest handprint.

the biggest handprint. Light shines brightest in the midst of darkness.

In the late 1990s nearly everyone remembers the looming threat of Y2K. No one knew for sure what would happen to the computerized world as the global clock blasted midnight into a new millennium. The predictions of ominous disaster were daunting. Many were scared to death not knowing if the threat was real. Numbers of books were written with predictions of transportation, communication and commerce coming to a screeching halt as computers around the world malfunctioned. Major international corporations spent millions of dollars upgrading computer systems and talk shows across the country hosted debates on the pending disaster.

Christian leaders responded in many ways as they desired to responsibly shepherd their people. As for me, I didn't know what to believe about it. On one hand I didn't want to overreact, but on the other hand if people where going to be in a position of suffering, I wanted our church to be on the frontline providing relief to their distress. After reading Shaunti Feldhahn's book, *Y2K: The Millennium Bug*, I was inspired to call the Red Cross of America and asked them what they thought about the reality of the situation. They held the same conviction that I did and were grateful for any help they could get. We set up a meeting with their staff and ours to discuss a possible action plan for our city. We established a partnership as a result of that meeting and our church took on the responsibility of setting up a crisis center. Over the next few months, the Red Cross trained our staff in crisis management. We then approached the church body with our plan and asked for their involvement and support.

Our church had already gained a reputation in the city as one of the most benevolent agencies. We had been feeding the homeless in the park every week for over 12 years and had been operating a large food pantry—so it was natural for us to think in terms of compassion and mercy. Over the course of the next year we actually built a 4,000 square foot benevolence center on our campus that became known as the Barnabas Center. We stocked the warehouse and walk-in freezer and refrigeration unit with food. We also set up a propane-driven generator system that would run our facilities during a power outage. We seized the moment and used the looming crisis to not only build a lasting relationship with the Red Cross, but a great facility that has served us ever since.

Though Y2K came and went with hardly a noticeable hiccup, we still have the Barnabas Center. Today, it houses a free medical clinic, a food pantry and warehouse that resource several other church food pantries, and is also used to train young mission students for crisis relief work around the world. Because of the ministry that happens at this facility, we have a reputation in our community that has given us amazing favor. For over eight years it has been run by an army of faithful volunteers who have provided food, medical aid and other forms of relief to thousands of poor people throughout the city.[1]

With God's grace and a vision for the future, we were able to take a potential looming disaster and use it to make a big handprint – one that continues to make an impression today.

Vision Takes Thought and Planning

Years ago, Nancy and I bought a fixer-upper house. Throughout our marriage, we purchased houses nobody wanted because we realized the value in sweat equity (especially since we didn't have much money!). We have learned to see potential in things most people would cast aside. As a result, when we bought this particular home, the wheels started turning. I began envisioning a long entry leading up to this house with trees that would produce a beautiful canopy stretching from one side of the driveway to the other. However, the thought of the work involved in this venture overwhelmed me. My vision quickly degenerated into images of me walking up and down the driveway with a water hose to ensure the trees' survival.

Unable to let my vision go and also unable to invest the time it would take daily to water the trees, I decided to develop a plan that would make this vision a reality. I made a list of all the things it would take for this tree-lined driveway to develop without my constant attention. I needed an irrigation system, which meant I needed to plan for its layout. I also needed the tools to accomplish this endeavor. After much thought and attention to detail, I dug a trench, laid the pipe and wiring system for a timed irrigation system and began planting trees. Instead of watering the trees each day, I would check on them once a week to make sure water was getting where it needed to go. After a while, the vision turned into reality. The trees flourished—and so did I as a result of good planning.

King Solomon knew a thing or two about good planning. Given the option of asking for anything he wanted, he asked for more wisdom. So, when King Solomon writes about wisdom, we should pay close attention. Consider what he says happens when we seek God for wisdom and understanding:

> Then you will understand what is right, just, and fair, and you will know how to find the right course of action every time. For wisdom will enter your heart, and knowledge will fill you with joy. Wise planning will watch over you. Understanding will keep you safe.
>
> — Proverbs 2:9-11

Winston Churchill, one of the great leaders of the 20th century, was a free flowing stream of ideas. But they weren't always the best ideas. Churchill's chief of staff, Alan Brooke, said, "Winston had ten ideas every day, one of which was good, and he did not know what it was." When it comes to developing plans, we ask God for his input and direction so that our plans aren't just our good ideas. That's why developing plans to execute vision happens best when it emerges out of a heart connected with God. I have ideas all the time, but I know I need to seek God and get his revelation in order for these plans to result in a big impact on the lives of those around me.

Here's what else King Solomon has to say on this important issue:

My child, don't lose sight of good planning and insight. Hang on to them, for they fill you with life and bring you honor and respect. They keep you safe on your way and keep your feet from stumbling. You can lie down without fear and enjoy pleasant dreams. You need not be afraid of disaster or the destruction that comes upon the wicked, for the Lord is your security. He will keep your foot from being caught in a trap.

— Proverbs 3:21-26

According to King Solomon, good planning results in some delicious fruit from which we all want to partake. He says, good planning …

* will fill you with life (vs. 22)
* will bring honor & respect (vs. 22)
* keep you safe & from stumbling (vs. 23)
* will help you sleep well (vs. 24)
* will prevent you from fearing pending disaster (vs. 25)
* will allow the Lord to be your advocate and keep you secure (vs. 26)
* keep you from getting caught in a trap (vs. 26)

If you want to have a simplified life that leaves a big impact on the world, you have to have a plan. There is no better time to get this concept than now. Just ask someone older than yourself about it. When you put off planning, a week turns into a month, months turn into years, and before you know it you're wondering what happened to your life. If that's not motivation enough, King Solomon says if you have a good plan, there are some great benefits that go along with it. Who would

> If you want to have a simplified life that leaves a big impact on the world, you have to have a plan.

not want any of the things he suggests are the result of good planning? Let's take a look at another king who understood the value of strategic planning.

Joseph: Our Biblical Example

Readiness provides security and peace not only in times of crisis, but also in times of plenty. King Hezekiah grasped this concept well, but he wasn't the only person in the Bible who understood the importance of being prepared. Let's take a look at some characteristics of preparedness that marked Joseph's life as he led the nation of Egypt through a massive change from limitless consumption to small footprint living. (see Genesis 41)

1. Joseph was no stranger to adversity. When adversity hits your life, you realize the smooth ride can often be bumpy—and the next time it happens, it's not such a shock. The first time Joseph found himself lying on the ground at the bottom of a pit, he probably was a little shaken to say the least. A few betrayals and a few years later, he understood what it took to make the best out of a bad situation.

2. Joseph was an organizer and administrator. For Joseph, administration came easy to him. He had no problems organizing and leading any group of people he was placed over, from prisoners to Potiphar's house to an entire nation. Being prepared means we need to develop basic organizational skills to some degree even if this doesn't come naturally to us.

3. Joseph was always aware of potential disaster. Getting thrown into a well surely caught Joseph off-guard, but he was on the lookout for possible roadblocks after that incident. The ability to sense potential problems—as well as listen to God's voice for warnings of impending doom—is what set Joseph apart. It's also what saved a nation or two. By having the awareness to detect possible disaster ahead and listen for God's voice on the matter, we will have the opportunity to get prepared.

4. Joseph understood timing and patience. He spent two years in prison after being falsely accused by Potipher's wife. Yet never do we hear him clamoring for justice. He quietly waits for God to open doors for him. We get into trouble when we try to press God on our situations. We can pray and ask him to change things—but ultimately, the perfect timing needs to remain in His hands so that doors don't just open, they fly open.

5. Joseph prepared in times of plenty. Instead of looking at a short track record of success, Joseph resisted the urge to indulge and instead prepared. His wisdom in doing so meant that when disaster struck, times weren't so bad for Egypt and some surrounding countries. Most people live without thought of the future or what might happen if disaster strikes. Living off what you need and saving the rest is a great way to be prepared for the unexpected.

6. Joseph's gift of simplicity brought blessings to others. Potipher, the chief jailer, Pharaoh—they all benefited from Joseph's ability to organize while making things simple and worry free. When we bring simplicity into the environment of those around us, we bring blessings to them. Life is easier around us—and simple.

God helped Joseph prepare an entire nation during seven years of abundance by storing excess food so that they could not only save their own people during the following seven years of drought and famine, but also the nation of Israel. Like the families that weathered Hurricane Katrina and quickly recovered from the crisis to help others, we want to be in a position of helping those less fortunate in their time of need as well.

The question you must ask yourself is: *Who will you look to for help in a time of disaster?* Or could you be so prepared that others look to you, giving you an opportunity to seize the moment and be the hands and feet of Jesus to people in desperate need? In order to pour out God's extravagant love on people, we must be prepared to serve at a moment's notice, which is much more possible when our lives are simplified and we've planned ahead.

The Fruit of Preparedness

As we begin moving down this path of planning and preparing, we must ask ourselves a few questions: Who or what is in control of our lives? Who is our master? Who or what do we look to for peace? Is it the God of peace or a world system that falsely promises the provisions for our security and comfort? Though I am not fanatic about this, I believe in being somewhat of a Boy Scout—be ready and prepared for the unexpected. This type of approach to life is directly related to the pursuit of a life of simplicity and peace.

Once while living on our old homestead, four feet of snow fell unexpectedly. People across our region went into a state of panic because they had been caught unprepared. The roads were closed for nearly two weeks and with them much of the power grid was shut down, resulting in a loss of electricity. Our family not only weathered those weeks, but we enjoyed them almost like a vacation. Our root cellar was stocked with preserved and dried food, we built fires with wood that had been cut and stored early that fall, and our home was independent from the commercial power grid. Our simple lifestyle allowed us to live in peace while others struggled and, in some cases, suffered. There is something deeply comforting to know that if things got bad due to any kind of physical or social malfunction, we aren't at the complete mercy of the world's provision.

In implementing this concept into your family's way of life, this is done best when everyone is on board. If you're married, husbands and wives have to embrace the challenge of preparedness together, involving their children and possibly their extended family as well. A plan should be put in place that allows everyone to participate. Recently, Nancy and I began recapturing our vision to get our home and life back to the basics again. We planted a small orchard of fruit trees, began raising chickens for eggs and designed a new vegetable garden in raised beds for higher productivity in a smaller space. We are also investigating the use of some of the new technologies in solar and wind power for our electrical needs. Not only are these sources of energy economical and self-sustaining, but they are renewable, natural and environmentally friendly. In addition, we have put a reserve water tank on the hill behind us for an emergency water supply in case of fire or power outage. When we shop, we not only buy food for our immediate needs, but we also try to add a few things to our storage pantry so that over time our reserve is built up. We find ourselves enjoying some of the innovative ideas in magazines like *Mother Earth News* and *Home Power*. Some of the concepts in these periodicals may seem a bit out there, but they present us with a creative challenge that is forward thinking and smart.

These changes are wholesale and not something I did in a day. In fact, many of the changes I've been able to make are due to my decision to live on a ranch outside the city. I understand that making the transition from the way most people in the western world live to a small footprint lifestyle can't happen immediately. Whether you are single or married, live in the suburbs, urban setting or rural areas, this process takes time. However, it can be done. Small steps over small periods of time equate to giant leaps over longer expanses of time.

Your Challenge: Make a Plan

So, what do you want to accomplish in this window of opportunity called life on this earth? This isn't about what you need, but about what you really want. How do you do it?

If you're from my generation, now is the time to ask yourself some questions, like, "How will I spend my golden years?" or "What will I do for the remainder of my years on earth?" If you're in your 20s or 30s, there are some more appropriate questions for you to ask yourself, such as, "What is my ultimate goal in life? What is holding me back from reaching it?" We must all ask ourselves if our life is too filled or too out of control. We must all question what the physical, emotional or spiritual clutter is in our lives that is rendering us ineffective.

So, what do you want? Where do you go from here?

You didn't get into your current situation now overnight, so don't expect to escape it overnight either. In our fast-food, I-want-it-now western culture, that whole concept of waiting and patience seems foreign. However, we must realize that these things take time. Plans develop slowly. But remember, we're building for the long haul.

When I taught through this series with our church, I challenged everybody to develop a seven-year plan for their lives. Think about where you want to be in seven years and answer these questions:

* What do you want to be doing seven years from now?
* What do you want to be different with your life seven years from now?
* What spiritual goals do you desire for your life within the next seven years? Emotional goals? Physical goals?
* How do you want to be impacting the community in which you live seven years from now?

Once you answer these questions while envisioning your life in seven years, begin working backward on each one. What do you need to do each year to reach that goal in seven years? For example, if you want to be a college professor and you have no PhD then you will need to develop a plan for getting into school and getting your degree first. If you want to be feeding 500 homeless people in your city each day but have no such outlet, you need to begin building toward that in some form or another. Maybe you start by cooking hamburgers in a local park on Saturdays and then expand what you're doing each year to include more people and more days. But you have to start somewhere.

Planning provides a course of action. It may take us years to accomplish the things we set out to do, but at least we know what steps we need to take to get there. Long ago we decided we wanted to serve the Lord in some capacity for the rest of our lives. At the same time we want the freedom to choose what that will look like for us. In working on a plan for financial freedom, we have greater peace and hopefully a more simplified retirement. When our investments begin to dominate our thinking and cause us to begin to fret, it's a warning that we may need to liquidate and simplify, even if it means receiving a lesser return on our money. We have found that monetary risk oftentimes spells anxiety and thus complicates our life. Therefore, Nancy and I are cautious not to let investments rob us of our focus. It is scriptural and wise for all of us to dream and plan for a secure financial future. If those plans are implemented wisely, they not only help provide a life of contentment but also lead us to greater simplicity.

I believe God honors small beginnings—and believe me, when you start trying to simplify your life for the purpose of being able to make a bigger impact, it takes more work than you can imagine. In fact, you might believe that you are going backwards for a while before you begin to progress towards your goals. However, we can't get anywhere without taking those initial steps toward making this a reality.

Questions to Ponder

1. In what ways have you prepared yourself and/or your family for the unexpected?

2. How do you intend on moving from a place of little or no preparation to a place of great preparation?

Small Footprint

Action point: Create a seven-year plan for your life based on what types of things you want to be doing and what type of life you want to be living, especially when it comes to other relationships, so...

Big Footprint

Action Point: ...you can work toward making a bigger impact in the lives of those around you as your plan begins to take shape.

Looking Back

* You didn't get into your current situation overnight, so don't expect to escape it overnight either. Start by making a seven-year plan.

* If you want to have a simplified life that leaves a big impact on the world, you have to have a plan.

* Planning provides a course of action. It may take us years to accomplish the things we set out to do, but at least we know what steps we need to take to get there.

conclusion

Beyond the Big Handprint

Reform yourself and the church—or languish in irrelevance

"Idealistic reformers are dangerous because their idealism has no roots in love, but is simply a hysterical and unbalanced rage for order amidst their own chaos."
– William Irwin Thompson

"I APPEAL to you therefore, brethren, and beg of you in view of [all] the mercies of God, to make a decisive dedication of your bodies [presenting all your members and faculties] as a living sacrifice, holy, devoted, consecrated and well pleasing to God, which is your reasonable (rational, intelligent) service and spiritual worship."
– Romans 12:1 (Amplified Bible)

L iving simply and loving extravagantly is the roadmap for us from this point forward. I hope you seriously ponder the words in this book and let them permeate your heart to such a depth that it changes the way you live because our hopeless world needs Christians to start acting Christ-like. The world is in crisis and there's no denying it. Most people know this but their behaviors belie their knowledge. Far too many people remain in a state of spiritual denial today, believing everything will always remain the same. I believe that if the truth were known in the heart of every true Christian, then a sense of pressure would begin growing. The present day global crisis could be categorized into seven general areas:

1. Spiritual deadness and confusion
2. Environmental decline
3. Disease, health and sanitation
4. World hunger
5. Human injustice
6. Illiteracy
7. Moral, visionary and organizational leadership

Some voices have said these social issues are not the business of the church, arguing that the church has been commissioned only to take the Gospel to all nations by baptizing, making disciples and teaching them all that Jesus taught. Others would say that discipleship is a verb; that it must show action and be every Christian's state of being. However, the message of the love of God can never simply say "be warm and be filled"—it must truly demonstrate God's love in practical and functional ways. James said this when he told us that faith without works is dead. (see James 2:26)

Millions of people around this world are spiritually confused; they have perceived much of the Christian faith as irrelevant and inward, thus not caring about the very things that are threatening human existence. They have seen the church as angry, divided and ineffective at a time when true Christianity is needed the most. As a result many people have resisted and even resented the evangelistic message. In the days ahead it will be Christian activism that will proclaim the Gospel message the loudest. The truth is that world crisis has provided Christianity an opportunity to rise up and become the bright and shining light that God intended it to be for all his people.

At this point, the global environment is in rapid decline; for example, polluted water kills thousands of people everyday. Water related diseases such as Cholera, Malaria and every other kind of diarrheal disease are deadlier than AIDS in the developing world. Simple sanitation training, well-drilling and stagnant water removal alone could save thousands of lives a day. Global warming is no longer just a concern but a reality. While many evangelicals are in a debate over why the world is warming (be it natural causes or human causes) the polar caps are rapidly melting, the Northwest Passage is ice free for the first time since the advent of satellite imaging, and ocean currents as well as the global climate are changing. Ocean levels are rising and affecting low lying regions of the world. Some of the more vulnerable places such as New Orleans, the United Kingdom and the Netherlands have invested billions of dollars already to combat the rising tide surges. Unfortunately, places such as Bangladesh can't afford these extensive engineering projects. Already Bangladesh's agriculture is being drastically affected by the increase of salt in fresh water irrigation systems. It is estimated that in the very near future they will be faced with the migration of millions of what has become known as "environmental refugees".

The idea that globalization would produce greater sources of affordable food and aid in world hunger has been proven to be false. The globalized market has become just a market that is economically driven by the bottom line of economic business. The price of food may be affordable for the average westerner who shops at super stores, but for the majority of the world who are surviving on less than two dollars a day, the ability to provide groceries is becoming more difficult by the day. Major corporations are moving the poor from the small village farm onto land that is less fertile with less access to water. Seventy percent of the fresh water on the earth is now being used for agriculture; global warming poses a growing concern and humanity is being faced with yet another new challenge.

Human injustice has been around as long as mankind, but today it is taking on a whole new face. Children soldiering in areas like the Congo and Sudan are beginning to get the attention of many; the growing modern day slave trade is hundreds of times worse than in the day of William Wilberforce. Each year over 17,000 people are brought to the United States against their will or under false pretense for human exploitation such as the sex market and sweat shop labor. Many are young girls 12 to 14 years old who have been promised a better life but are sold into a hopeless life of bondage and pain.

The lack of education in many parts of the world is a major cause of illiteracy which fuels the fires of poverty. Illiteracy creates an environment in which entire cultures of people are vulnerable to extreme poverty and human exploitation.

Spiritual deadness has a way of turning the hearts of people cold. Many with this condition of the heart are those who have risen to positions of national and world leadership. Without Christ as the center of a leader's value structure they become self absorbed, self-promoting and strive to merely secure positions of power and wealth. Leaders unmotivated by the heart of God, which encompasses true compassion and mercy, may only perpetuate the poverty, struggles and atrocities that escalate the suffering condition of humanity. In these situations human life is considered only as a means to gain greater control and power. These conditions often breed rebellion and violence from within, stirring up armies of angry terrorists indoctrinated with hatred causing more suffering for those caught in the middle.

In nearly every case it is the poor who suffer first, the very ones who Jesus commanded us to care for first. The world needs a church that is unified, equipped and empowered to take the true message of God's unending love right into the very middle of the turmoil and crisis. Consider what could happen if one third of the world population that proclaims Christ as savior would rise up in unity and address these life threatening issues. The church is a potential workforce of over two billion people. It is staggering to think what could be accomplished if Christians everywhere embraced the reality of the commission Jesus gave us of caring for those in need. If there is to be reformation on this planet, the church must experience it first, and be willing to impact the world with the handprint of a loving, caring God. The church is the hope.

Based on the apostle Paul's teaching in Romans 12, here are the four steps I propose the church and Christians everywhere need to take in order to experience the type of reformation that leaves a big handprint of God's love on a world crying out for hope.

Four steps to reformation and the Big Handprint

Step #1: Consecration

Consecration is primarily an Old Testament word but can be overlaid on the New Testament concept of fully giving ourselves to the purposes of Christ. Consecration speaks of a willful decision to commit oneself to God. It literally means "to set something apart as holy and committed to the purposes of God." Read Paul's statement here as it is recorded in Romans 12:1 in the Amplified Bible; "I APPEAL to you therefore, brethren, and beg of you in view of [all] the mercies of God, to make a decisive dedication of your bodies [presenting all your members and faculties] as a living sacrifice, holy, devoted, consecrated and well pleasing to God, which is your reasonable (rational, intelligent) service and spiritual worship."

Consecration is the first step of the journey to true reformation and it first requires an awakening to the reality and presence of God.

It is dependent upon a person's personal recognition of God's empowering presence in their life, a need for repentance from the things that has separated them from God (i.e. sin) and a willful choice to accept his rule and reign. It is the process of receiving Christ both as Lord and savior. It is the first and most important step in the Christian journey and becoming an instrument of reform.

Step #2: Transformation

Transformation is an issue of the mind. It is the process of coming into a new worldview. It speaks of no longer seeing the world the way the rest of the world does, but rather through the eyes of God. It is referred to as "Kingdom perspective". It is diametrically opposed to the old way of seeing things. It is part of an upside down world; one in which the least is the greatest, the first is the last, we are to love our enemies, and the leader is called to servant-hood. Paul said it like this, "Don't copy the behavior and customs of this world, but let God transform you into a new person by changing the way you think. Then you will learn to know God's will for you, which is good and pleasing and perfect." (Romans 12:2)

Transformation is the process of grasping God's perspective not only for the world, but for your own life. It is coming into the reality that your life isn't an accident, but rather perfectly designed and planned. It is the awareness of the fact, as Rick Warren said, "You were created for a purpose." The charismatic expression of Christianity has referred to this phase as "renewal" because it is renewing your mind by opening your eyes to who you are and why you were put on earth at this particular time in human history. The NIV translates this, "but be transformed by the renewing of your mind." Renewal is not revival as many have hoped, but instead can lead to revival if the process doesn't stop there. Renewal is an inward work of the Holy Spirit; it is a healing work that encompasses the hope that the renewed believer will discover God's good, pleasing and perfect will for their individual life. Revival, on the other hand, is an outward work of Christ moving through an empowered Christian. It is a result of people who have experienced renewal and discovered why God created them—and they are willing to go do it.

Step #3: Sanctification

Sanctification is the process by which God makes us more like him. It is the process of becoming Christ-like in our attitudes and actions. It is a deep work of the Holy Spirit that does the final preparations to ready us for his service. It is here that he puts a holy righteous passion in us for a lost and dying world. It is here that he renders our hearts to see the world the way he sees it and gives us not only the desire to do something about it, but empowers our gifts and abilities to be effective. Sanctification not only gets our eyes off ourselves, but first allows us to take an honest evaluation of who we are, measuring not only our level of faith but also our deficits. It is at this point that we are motivated to get anything out of our lives that might hold us back from being functional Kingdom vessels. Paul said it this way in Romans 12. "I give each of you this warning: Do not think you are better than you really are. Be honest in your evaluation of yourselves, measuring yourselves by the faith God has given us. Just as our bodies have many parts and each part has a special function, so it is with Christ's body."

Before I was in full time ministry I was a secondary school teacher. One of the subjects I taught during my twelve years in public education was anatomy and physiology. I was fascinated with the miracle of the body's systems, one of which was the nervous system. I learned a term there that has stuck with me ever since—*synapse*. Synapse refers to a miraculous electrical connection that transmits messages from the sensory nerves and the motor nerves. The sensory nerves transmit messages from the sensory organs, (the nose to smell, ears to hear, eyes to see, the tongue for taste and the skin for touch). This information from the outside world is brought to the central nervous system (CNS) as information so that the body might react to it. For example, we touch something hot and the sensory nerves transmit this message to the CNS so that synapse can take place allowing the motor nerves to stimulate the muscle fiber to pull away so as not to get burned.

Without synapse there is no response to the information gained. In my mind this is a perfect picture of many Christians who gain much knowledge but whose life reactions do not respond. As a result many Christians get burned by the world. Sanctification is like synapse. It makes our spirits sensitive to the pain and darkness of the world so that we will respond correctly.

God has given all of us certain gifts and abilities so that we can fulfill the reason he put us on the earth. Sanctification makes us acutely aware of this and motivates us to find our gifts and use our lives for his purposes. You can read about this in Romans 12:6-8. This is where Christian maturity and authenticity begin to take place.

Step #4: Reformation

Reformation means *to re-form* or *to form again*. In Jeremiah 18 the Lord spoke to the prophet concerning the reformation of his people. The Lord spoke to Jeremiah telling him to go down to the potter's shed where he would find a potter forming a clay jar. The scripture tells us in verse four that "the jar he (the potter) was making did not turn out as he had hoped, so he crushed it into a lump of clay again and started over." God is in the business of reformation. He loves to recreate, restore and reconcile. The concept of being "born again" or making an "old man into a new creation" is a clear picture of this supernatural process. The idea of being a clay jar that is crushed and reformed is not a very appealing picture and will be resisted by many. However, in reality this is the business God is in and a process every true believer must accept and embrace if they are truly sincere about becoming active functional vessels in God's Kingdom. Not only are we to do this on an individual level, but we must be willing to let it happen to us on a corporate church level. It is through this process that we will be ready and equipped to leave a big hand-print of God on a dying world. Only in this way will there ever be hope for social reformation. True reformers are people who embrace change—first in their own lives and then in the world around them.

In the Romans 12 dissertation, Paul gives us a picture of what this reformed person will look like and how he will behave. He writes, "Don't just pretend to love others. Really love them. Hate what is wrong. Hold tightly to what is good. Love each other with genuine affection, and take delight in honoring each other. Never be lazy, but work hard and serve the Lord enthusiastically. Rejoice in our confi-dent hope. Be patient in trouble, and keep on praying. When God's people are in need, be ready to help them. Always be eager to prac-tice hospitality. Bless those who persecute you. Don't curse them; pray that God will bless them. Be happy with those who are happy, and weep with those who weep. Live in harmony with each other. Don't be too proud to enjoy the company of ordinary people. And don't think you know it all! Never pay back evil with more evil. Do things in such a way that everyone can see you are honorable. Do all that you can to live in peace with everyone" (Romans 12:9-18).

Reformers are people who have first allowed God to reform them. They are the ones who have captured the attributes of Christ and are motivated to bring these characteristics to a lost and dying world. They have become both "God-centered" and "others-centered". As Paul put it, they are people who have truly come to a place of humil-ity and because of it they no longer look out for merely their own interests, but now have a sincere interest in others, seeing them as more important than themselves. They are people who have the same attitude as Christ Jesus. (see Philippians 2:1-4) This is a picture of someone who has rendered his life down to the things that are impor-tant to God. This is the small footprint.

A reformer is an agent of social change, a person who will never be satisfied with a complacent status quo society that's destined for destruction. A reformer is a fighter who has the heart of a Spirit-filled warrior. They are not overwhelmed with hopelessness and despair, but have received the call to place themselves on the very front lines of a world in crisis, seeing it as Kingdom opportunity. They have embraced the adventure. They are people who believe that God delights in doing extraordinary things with ordinary people – if they will have the faith to believe it and a willingness to step out. They are naturally supernatural people believing that they don't need to be super heroes; they are simply normal people who are willing to believe God to work through the gifting he has already placed in them. They have captured his heart of compassion, mercy and justice for a dark and broken world and want to make a difference with the life they've been given. They are willing to make the transition from a consumer lifestyle to a life of simplicity and meaning in an effort to make a small footprint. They do this so that they might be free and empowered to make a big handprint, leaving the world a better place because of the divine gift of life that they have been given.

If this idea is stirring in you and you want to do something about it, I want to invite you to join us by visiting www.reform-now.org. As these ideas have germinated, we want to give you a practical pathway to move from being a follower of Christ whose heart is moved with compassion and mercy for the world's crisis to an empowered person who has the knowledge and skills necessary to take appropriate action. We look forward to connecting with you and hearing your story as you join us in changing the world.

Big Footprint

Action Point: Go to www.reform-now.org and sign up for our newsletter and learn ways you can be a reformer in your community through leaving a big handprint.

Notes

Chapter One

[1] To learn more about your carbon footprint and calculate the one you're leaving on the earth, visit www.carbonfootprint.com

Chapter Two

[1] From the Fermi Project's Q Conference (www.fermiproject.com) in Atlanta, Ga., in April 2006. To learn more about Kevin Kelly and his futurist ideas, visit www.kk.org

Chapter Three

[1] "Victims of Trafficking and Violence Protection Act of 2000: Trafficking in Persons Report 2007." U.S. Department of State. http://www.state.gov/g/tip/rls/tiprpt/2007/

[2] To learn more about these organizations and get involved with them, find them on the web at the following sites:
Floresta - www.floresta.org
Seeds of Hope - www.sohip.org

Chapter Four

[1] In 2005, our church started a ministry designed to serve the environmental issues in our area and around the world called, "Let's Tend the Garden." If you are interested in this, I encourage you to visit our website www.letstendthegarden.org and learn more about it. You can also get more information about our annual conference designed to equip and train churches to care for the environment in their cities.

Chapter Five

[1] Our church has used many different programs to educate people about how to get out of debt and live a debt-free lifestyle, but Dave Ramsey's Financial Peace University has produced the best results of anything we've ever used. If you're interested in attending one of

these classes, visit www.daveramsey.com/fpu/home to search for a class that is being held in your community.

Chapter Six
[1] Luke 4:18

[2] "For the wages of sin is death, but the gift of God is eternal life in Christ Jesus our Lord" (Romans 6:23); and "A dog returns to its vomit" and "A sow that is washed goes back to her wallowing in the mud" (2 Peter 2:22).

[3] "The Multitasking Generation" by Claudia Wallis, *Time* magazine, March 20, 2006.

Chapter Seven
[1] To learn more about the Barnabas Center, visit our website www.vineyardboise.org

Discussion
Guide

Chapter One: Small Footprint

This chapter focuses on the importance of reducing our physical footprint through simple living. *Simple living* is a lifestyle that allows us to focus on the things that are most important to us, such as relationships both inside and outside of our families, without being encumbered by an inordinate amount of responsibilities that demand our attention. (pg. 20) Our footprint is the stamp left behind through our lifestyle, which consists of both our material possessions and the way we steward our time on earth.

Additional Reading: 2 Corinthians 11

Questions:
1. In your current living environment, what are some practical steps you can take to shrink your footprint?

2. Has shrinking your "footprint" ever been important to you before? Why or why not?

3. How does a smaller footprint honor God?

4. If leaving a smaller footprint is about creating space in your life to do things that matter, what are some of the things that matter to you that you would like to do?

Notes

Chapter Two: Big Handprint

This chapter focuses on the importance of leaving a big handprint on the world around us. Leaving a big handprint occurs when we make ourselves available to be used by God for his plans and purposes. (pg. 31) Making a big handprint with your life also means that with all that you do, you have one eye on eternity, realizing that the things you do today impact tomorrow.

Additional Reading: Romans 12

Questions:

1. Have there ever been periods in your life that you now wish you had that time back? If so, what led you down that path? What would you do differently today?

2. When you think about the future, do you think about it with hope or despair? Why?

3. What kind of impact do you think you can have on the future of the current environment and culture in which you live? What is driving you to make a difference?

4. If you were to reduce your footprint today, in what areas of change and influence would you be able to be involved? How would that impact the world around you? How would it influence others?

Notes

Chapter Three: Pathway to Adventure

This chapter deals with the adventure that all of us want in life. Unfortunately, our culture has convinced us that adventure can be found in stockpiling our money, buying huge houses, driving fancy cars, and wielding power and fame. This mis-adventure drives people into despair as they realize the dream they chased was empty. However, real adventure rests within the heart of every man and woman willing to give their lives away to others that demonstrates the compassionate heart of Christ.

Additional Reading: Luke 9:51-62

Questions:

1. In what ways have you experienced adventure in your life? Was it fulfilling? Exciting?

2. What excites you when you wake up each day? What are those moments where you experience sheer joy?

3. How ᵎave you taken advantage of a crisis in your community by showing others the love of Christ in a difficult time? What were the results?

4. The Christian life is a life of activism based on biblical principal, and if we don't respond to the brokenness of the world in some way, nothing will ever change. (pg. 51) In what ways do you feel stirred to respond to the brokenness in the world today?

Notes

Chapter Four: A Simple Solution

This chapter deals with the one solution to the two commissions God gave us: Care for the earth and make disciples. Our planet is fragile and delicately woven together by the Creator, yet people have ignored the warning signs of our hurting planet in favor of creating more goods that find a fast track to overflow from landfills, but leave people empty inside. (pgs. 55-56) Followers of Jesus are able to solve so many issues when they are united in their love for God and each other.

Additional Reading: Luke 5:1-11

Questions:

1. In what ways have you engaged in caring for the environment? How does your common love for God's creation encourage you in this?

2. If you have broken status quo in any group you've been a part of, what has the reaction been like? What type of struggle did you face internally in doing so? What emboldened your decision to go against the grain?

3. How do you express your love for others in ways that encourages them and reminds them of God's love for them?

4. Take a moment to think about what you would like your life to be remembered for. What would you want your epitaph to say?

Notes

Chapter Five: Less External Complexity

This chapter talks about how the complex nature of our lifestyles can make it difficult to leave a big handprint and love others extravagantly. If you want to figure out what's actually important to you instead of what you say is important, just look at how you spend two things: your time and your money. (pg. 70)

Additional Reading: Luke 16:1-13

Questions:

1. In taking stock of how you spend your time and money, what does it reflect about what you think is important? Is that what you really want to be the most important in your life?

2. How has your life been impacted through the complexity of financial stresses and time pressures?

3. What steps have you taken in the past or could you take now to reduce that complexity? How can others in community with you help you execute your ideas?

4. If you had more time and energy, where would you focus it? How would it impact your life today and those around you?

Notes

Chapter Six: Less Internal Complexity

This chapter talks about how when we become complex on the inside, it is difficult to connect with God and hear his voice for our lives. We've got to get beyond ourselves and let Jesus have his way with our lives. We must quit bemoaning our situation and take advantage of the provision made available to us through the cross. We have to start living like a new creation for creation's sake. (pg. 84-85)

Additional Reading: James 4:1-10

Questions:

1. How difficult is it for you to escape the pressure society puts on everyone to look out for "number one"? In what ways do you resist this idea? In what ways do you succumb to it?

2. What is your biggest obstacle to peace in your soul right now? How must you navigate around it?

3. A broken heart is broken soil, a place where life can spring forth when tended properly. How will you allow your heart to be broken so that it may produce life? How can those in community with you help you in this process?

4. Of the spiritual disciples of solitude, prayer, reading the Bible, and fellowship, community and service, which is most difficult for you? Why? How can you strengthen these disciplines in your life?

Notes

Chapter Seven: More Preparedness

This chapter gives us a clear understanding of how when we're prepared and willing to show God's extravagant love when a crisis hits, we can. Difficulty most often sets a stage of opportunity for those who desire to make the biggest handprint. Light shines brightest in the midst of darkness. (pg. 102-103)

Additional Reading: Genesis 41

Questions:
1. If disaster struck your community today, what preparations have you made that would enable you to help? How could you help?

2. Are there things you would like to be able to do in the future in case disaster struck your area or another region of the world and needed help? If so, what would that be?

3. What type of foresight is necessary for you to pull of your ideas of helping in the future? Training? Finances?

4. How will your preparedness for future crisis be a blessing to others? What would you like to see happen as a result of your preparedness in the lives of those you help?

Notes

Conclusion: Beyond the Big Handprint

The conclusion is a challenge for us to become change agent or reformers within our communities and local churches. Over the past few years, Christianity in the west has become so inwardly focused that the church is missing the greatest opportunity to administer the Gospel and share the love of Christ the world has ever known. A reformer is an agent of social change, a person who will never be satisfied with a complacent status quo society that's destined for destruction. (pg. 124-125)

Additional Reading: Jeremiah 18:1-17

Questions:
1. In what ways can you become a reformer in your church or community? What areas of influence do you have that you can begin to call others to make a difference with their lives?

2. In the four-step process of consecration, transformation, sanctification and reformation, where are you? What has been your experience in that process?

3. How have you embraced reformation in your own heart as a result of reading through this book?

4. Of all the topics discussed in this book, what has prompted you to make the biggest change in the way you live? Why?

Notes

RE:FORM

To learn more about RE:FORM, visit our new website at

www.reform-now.org

This local church-based non-profit organization is addressing seven of the world's greatest crisis through training, equipping, empowering, and sending people out to make a difference. Our website shares the stories of those who have taken seriously this charge to change the world. Through blogs, articles, videos and newsletters, you'll be able to learn more about what we're doing and how you can take it back to your church and community.

ABOUT THE AUTHOR

Tri Robinson is the founding pastor of the Vineyard Boise Church in Boise, Idaho, a growing fellowship of over 3,000. He is the author of *Saving God's Green Earth* and *Revolutionary Leadership*. Tri and his wife, Nancy, live in Sweet, Idaho, and have two grown children, Kate and Brook.

OTHER BOOKS BY TRI ROBINSON

Revolutionary Leadership
by Tri Robinson
retail price: $12.95

Is your church growing? More importantly, is your church creating authentic followers of Jesus? In *Revolutionary Leadership*, author and pastor Tri Robinson shares his journey of planting a church that is serious about discipleship. Out of his desire to pastor a church that was intentional and successful at developing passionate followers of Jesus, Robinson discovered the concept of synergy and how its components can help revolutionize leadership within a church.

Saving God's Green Earth
by Tri Robinson
retail price: $12.95

For hundreds of years, the church championed the beauty of God's creation, demonstrating in many ways how it points to the Creator. However, over the last century, the evangelical church has let the value of caring for creation slip away. Author Tri Robinson makes a compelling case for the biblical mandate behind environmental stewardship and shows the church what it can do about this eroding value.

Through sharing both his own personal story and the story of his church in response to environmental concerns, Robinson clearly shows how important this value is and how effective it is in showing others the Creator. Not only does Robinson inspire the reader to care for the environment, he reveals a clear pathway to making the value of environmental stewardship real in both the life of the reader and the Christian community in which he or she is involved.

Sample chapters and these books are available for purchase at: www.ampelonpublishing.com/store